AMPIONSHIP
FRED CURRY

NES ★ GIRLS

MISS LEMKE

5—SCICLUNA
EX. MATSUOKA
KIDS $1.00 GENS.
★★★★★★★★★
STAR WRESTLING

RENA   JULY
        26TH

PIONSHIP

OHNNY BAREND

s. THE CURRYS
FATHER & SON TEAM

G BILL MILLER
RENE COULET

HRILLER

RAY STEVENS & PETER MAIVIA
WORLDS CHAMPIONS

★★★★★★★★★★★★★★

Collins vs Steamboat ★ SHIBUYA vs PEDRO

★★★★★★★★★★★★★★★★
INTERNATIONAL ALL STAR WRESTLING
WED. **HIC ARENA** SEPT. 20TH
WORLD'S CHAMPIONSHIP

BOCK & STEVENS vs. PEDRO & WAHOO

—STEEL ESCAPE PROOF CAGE—

ED FRANCIS vs. FRED BLASSIE

WED. BIG TIME WRESTLING MAR. 8TH

SAT
TER

WORLDS CHAMPIONSHIP

JOHNNY BAREND vs. DORY FUNK
HAWAIIAN CHAMPIONSHIP

ED FRANCIS   VS.   GENE KINISKI

MADDOG MAYNE vs. RIPPER COLLINS

SIKI vs IAUKEA   GRAHAM vs. CARSO

Gentleman ED FRANCIS Presents

50th STATE BIG TIME WRESTLING!

Gentleman ED FRANCIS Presents

50th STATE BIG TIME WRESTLING!

 **By Edmund C. Francis**

with Larry Fleece

WATERMARK
PUBLISHING

ISBN 978-1-935690-24-5

Library of Congress Control Number: 2012951914

Design and production
Leo Gonzalez
Angela Wu-Ki

Photo credits
Personal photos from the Francis family collection, wrestling photos by George Beppu and wrestling memorabilia courtesy of Bill Atkinson (50thstatebigtimewrestling.com)
pp. 5, 29, 125 bottom, "KGMB-9 Remembers Wrestling in Hawaii," Lawrence E. Pacheco, producer, © 2000 Lee Enterprises, Inc.
p. 7, 12, 23, 25, 101 right, *Honolulu Advertiser, Honolulu Star-Bulletin*

pp. 14, 91, Tracy Capello/Ventres family archives

p. 24, Desoto Brown Collection

p. 44, Irving Rosen/Bishop Museum

pp. 61, 70, 71 right, 72, 102, 107, Annie Lum Barend

p. 79, Brian Roache

p. 84, *Baltimore Sun*/Tribune Photo Archives

p. 112, *Chicago Sun-Times*

p. 118, *World Wrestling*

p. 156, *Hawaii Wrestling Review*

Watermark Publishing
1088 Bishop Street, Suite 310
Honolulu, Hawai'i 96813
Telephone 1-808-587-7766
Toll-free 1-866-900-BOOK
sales@bookshawaii.net
www.bookshawaii.net

Printed in Korea

Contents

Foreword

Gentleman Ed Francis Presents 50th State Big Time Wrestling! is the product of a series of lengthy conversations I had with Ed in the summer of 2012 at his daughter Pixie's home outside Kansas City, Kansas.

Prior to my time visiting and chatting with Ed, he and Pixie had already begun laying the foundation for the book. In earlier talks with his daughter, Ed had recalled a variety of remarkable stories from his colorful past as a youngster growing up in Depression-era Chicago, as a pro wrestler crisscrossing the mainland U.S. and, ultimately, as the promoter of 50th State Big Time Wrestling in Hawaii.

Pixie had ably and skillfully transcribed many of Ed's recollections, and it is her fine work that served as the launching pad for this book focusing on Ed's years in the Islands. My sincere thanks go out to Pixie for all her labors.

My interest in the project stemmed from my own years growing up in Hawaii, watching Gentleman Ed and Lord Tally Ho Blears on KGMB-TV, either calling the wild wrestling matches or conducting those crazy locker-room interviews with Ripper Collins, Handsome Johnny Barend, Curtis "The Bull" Iaukea and all the rest.

I wasn't quite sure what to expect as we began the work. But soon after 86-year-old Ed Francis welcomed me into their home, I was astonished at his ability to recall events, names and even the smallest details from his time in Hawaii some 50 years earlier.

Beyond Ed's acuity of mind, he remains a powerful, physically imposing presence. In the room where we chatted, there was a weight bench and barbell set close at hand. Even at age 86, Ed continues to stay strong and fit.

Granted, some of our days started a bit later than others. Those were the days when Ed's knees, hips, shoulders and back reminded him of the brutal toll his chosen wrestling profession had taken on his body over the years.

But in getting the opportunity to spend time with Gentleman Ed, I was struck by something more than Ed's uncanny ability to bring to mind all the wonderful stories that fill this book. It was even more than his enduring, impressive physical stature.

What struck me most was the unmistakable quiet grace and dignity that Ed Francis retains to this day. It's a quality that likely led to his apt "Gentleman" moniker so many years earlier. It's a quality that allowed him to be the steady guiding hand through those roller-coaster years of wrestling's heyday in Hawaii.

Ed and I had lots of laughs recalling his days in the Islands, days that included a match with a 500-pound bear, a riot at the Civic Auditorium on King Street, threats to Don Ho, Johnny Barend's lit cigar sticking out of a coffin in the locker room and Ripper Collins' naked butt on display for all to see in the ring.

But there were a few tears as well. Ed welled up with emotion when he recalled Barend arriving in court to stick up for his friend Neff Maiava on trial. And Ed's memory of the sudden death of wrestler Jim Hady, a close friend of his, was a painful one.

The days of regional wrestling promoters like Gentleman Ed, crafting a sports entertainment

product designed specifically for a local audience, are likely behind us. As such, *Gentleman Ed Francis Presents 50th State Big Time Wrestling!* represents a singular slice of history, a snapshot of the days when the fervor of Island wrestling fans led to sold-out houses at the Civic and the Honolulu International Center Arena.

As you'll see in the pages that follow, the love that Hawaii fans had in the 1960s and '70s for the sport of pro wrestling was the direct result of the dedication of one man.

That man had come from abject poverty, charity bread lines and public housing as a child. He found sanctuary at the gym, and by building his muscles he built a career. Then he took an enormous gamble, betting it all on his dream of promoting his sport of wrestling in Hawaii.

Gentleman Ed Francis, Parkville, Missouri ca. 1998

That man's bet paid off. He lived his unique version of the American dream in the Islands, thrilling audiences every week and giving us all a show we'd never forget.

That man is Gentleman Ed Francis. I'm honored to call him my friend.

—Larry Fleece
Valencia, California

Introduction

For the past several years, the routine had been pretty much the same. I would stop into my dad's room every night before bedtime. We'd watch a few minutes of TV, chat about my day at work and the latest news, and maybe make up a story about what our two dogs were thinking as they lay like lumps at his feet. These were typical days in this small Kansas town; a man living out his retirement years in a modest room with a pile of history books and an old television set for company.

But something was brewing. I wasn't sure what it was, but it was palpable and restless. Dad was thinking about something, and I knew shortly I would be called to aid in whatever scheme he had cooking up in that amazingly sharp and creative 86-year-old mind of his. And then it happened. Sitting in his worn-out overstuffed chair, the pipe smoke curling above him, he turned down the sound on the TV and started to talk—a lot.

Opposite: Pixie Francis and brother Ed, Jr. (back row, far right) on the "Checkers and Pogo" television show

The stories started pouring out: a flood of memories dating as far back as 80 years to his childhood on the streets of Chicago; stories about family; about his loves; and of course Hawaii wrestling—his first love. One name reminded him of another and another, and the detail was infinite. That's when it hit me: This is a book; a fascinating sum of all the parts that made up a life that cannot be duplicated.

A year of Sundays later, what started as a flood of memories was transcribed into a word document, without a "home." That was until we were fortunate enough to make contact with an accomplished writer named Larry Fleece.

Aside from his natural ability, Larry was a perfect fit. He had grown up in Hawaii. Who better to bring this all to life than a man who had watched Gentleman Ed and Lord Tally Ho Blears shape the Hawaii television landscape of the 1960's and 70's? Who better than a guy who had watched Ripper Collins mispronounce Maui as "Mooey"? Yep, this was our man.

The result of Ed and Larry's collaboration is a collection of some of the most enduring memories of my youth and the lives of many others who shared in that unique time: *Gentleman Ed Francis Presents 50th State Big Time Wrestling!* The stories are from the inside out, meaning from the only man who knows how it all came to be, the guy who created it from a $10,000 loan and a homemade wrestling ring—Gentleman Ed himself.

In fact, it was the interest and efforts of a good many people that really brought this book to life. Duane Kurisu and George Engebretson of Watermark Publishing made this book possible through their belief in preserving such an important part of Hawaii's wrestling history for all of us to keep and enjoy. George Beppu and Bill Atkinson, who were instrumental in supplying many of the photos in this book, have with great pride spent countless hours cataloging some of the finest wrestling moments ever. Annie Barend sent us personal

August 28, 1969

pictures of Handsome Johnny Barend, never before seen in print. And, of course, there were the many fans who sent us well wishes and encouragement via our website, www.gentlemanedfrancis.com.

For my part, I am truly blessed to have been involved with this whole experience. I recall the day when, as a child, I met Andre the Giant in our kitchen and the time I swam with midget wrestlers in our family pool. Now I sit here writing an intro-duction to my dad's book. Go figure.

Funny how things work out. My dad still says the book was my idea, but you know what? The great promoters always let you think it was your idea. Right, Meestah Francis?

—Pixie Francis
Overland Park, Kansas

In the early 1960s the popular Civic Auditorium was the venue for one of the wildest brawls in Hawaii sports history—between fans of Curtis "The Bull" Iaukea and Neff Maiava (opposite left and right in 2001).

CHAPTER 1

Front-Page News

Is it possible that it was more than 50 years ago?

The headline that stretched across the front page of the *Honolulu Star-Bulletin* on Thursday, Aug. 17, 1961, told the story: "Wrestling Fans Battle Police in Civic Brawl."

The paper arrived with a "thud" outside my tiny office in the Civic Auditorium at 1314 S. King St., as we were still picking up the pieces from the fight the night before.

It had been a standing-room-only house inside the Civic for one of our regular Wednesday-night matches. The fans had all turned out on this warm August night in Honolulu for something special in the main event: a grudge match between the contender, local Hawaiian wrestler Curtis "The Bull" Iaukea, and the title holder, Samoan Neff Maiava, for the Hawaiian Heavyweight Wrestling Championship.

The match was a classic battle between the two big men, with both wrestlers scoring their points, delivering blows and taking plenty of punishment along the way. But the turning point in the match came when both men spilled out of the ring and onto the cement floor of the old Civic, not far from where I stood, keeping a watchful eye on the fan reaction to the bout that I had been building up and promoting for weeks.

The champ, Maiava, had the challenger,

Iaukea, backed up against one of the metal poles supporting the ring. Maiava moved in to finish off the challenger, and went to deliver his trademark "coconut head butt" with his thick Samoan skull.

But Iaukea ducked and dodged out of the way, and I heard the roar of the fans and their stunned reaction as Maiava smashed his head against the metal post that had been behind Iaukea. The blow knocked Maiava unconscious and sent him crashing like dead weight onto the floor of the Civic.

As the champ lay out cold on the cement, the ref counted him out of the match. Iaukea claimed the gold-buckled Hawaiian Championship belt, strapped it around his belly and strutted like a big, preening mynah bird in front of the fans.

That's when the real trouble began.

When Iaukea headed to the dressing room,

20 or so angry fans—supporters of the former champ, Maiava, rushed Curtis "The Bull" and tried to knock him down. I helped Iaukea hurry to the locker room, where we slammed the door behind him to try to protect him.

But the fans of Maiava kept coming. They picked up a wooden bench and began using it like a battering ram to get to Iaukea in the locker room. I got some help from Honolulu Police Sergeant Arnold Capellas, on duty in the auditorium, and we tried our best to push the fans back. But we were badly outnumbered. The angry crowd used a bank of four chairs strung together to force us back, instead, and they pinned me and Sergeant Capellas against the apron of the wrestling ring.

We found ourselves in full hand-to-hand combat, fighting and hitting these guys to keep them engaged until more police arrived.

Now the fans of the new champ, Iaukea, stepped into the fray, to meet the mayhem that Maiava's fans were creating. From where I stood, pinned against the ring, I watched as in just seconds the entire Civic Auditorium became a blizzard of flying metal folding chairs, cups, ice, floor and ceiling tiles—anything the fans could throw that wasn't bolted down.

I had suspected that something like this might happen. Bad blood had been simmering for weeks between Maiava and Iaukea—a fact, I must admit, I hadn't been shy about promoting—and I figured that it was only a matter of time before the Samoan and Hawaiian supporters of the two wrestlers might get a little too "involved."

That's why, in advance of Wednesday night's Hawaiian Championship match, I had asked Honolulu Police Department (HPD) for some extra manpower at the Civic. They had obliged, so when the chaos broke out, there were some additional plainclothes HPD officers in the audience. One of the officers at the Civic that night was none other than Captain Curtis P. Iaukea, watching his son wrestle for and win the title.

But even my "planted" cops weren't enough. Reinforcements were called, and pretty soon as many as two dozen of Honolulu's finest from the Metro and Vice divisions were battling the crowd, many of whom had turned on and started punching the officers. Even the head of the Metro squad, Larry Mehau, was trading punches in the arena when his division was deployed.

Right in the middle of the battle, an HPD cop named Larry Tuufuli had his pistol knocked from its holster, and it slid across the floor of the Civic. One of our wrestlers, Luigi Macera, saw the whole thing happen. He dashed in, grabbed the gun and hustled it into our locker

The grudge match between the Hawaiian Iaukea (opposite left) and the Samoan Maiava (opposite right) turned ugly when each wrestler's fans became directly involved in the proceedings.

9 Arrested as Ice, Cups, Chairs Fly

Wrestling Fans Battle Police in Civic Brawl

A screaming, chair-throwing brawl erupted at the Civic Auditorium last night after a wrestling match.

Three persons suffered possible skull fractures. One policeman was dazed by a hurled missile. Another was struck with a concrete tile. Brawlers tried to batter down the locker room door with a wooden bench.

ARRESTED

Nine persons were arrested. One brawler snatched a crutch from a cripple and used it as a club. The brawl began at about 10 p.m.—a minute after Curtis Iaukea won the Hawaiian heavyweight wrestling championship from Neff Maiava.

Iaukea is the son of Police Captain Curtis P. Iaukea, who was in the auditorium. Wearing his championship wrestling belt, Iaukea was walking toward his

Curtis Ioukea

dressing room when fans began shouting.

There was a surge toward Iaukea, and about 20 persons tried to knock him down.

Police Sergeant Arnold Capellas and Patrolman Larry Goeas tried to restore order on the ramp leading to the locker room but they were jumped by enraged fans.

Iaukea ran inside the locker room and slammed the door.

Yelling men picked up a wooden bench and battered at the door.

Two members of the police Metro Squad and two vice squadsmen in the audience rushed to the aid of the two uniformed patrolmen.

Reinforcements were called, and two dozen officers were embattled before the brawl was quelled 15 minutes after it started.

Metro Squadsman Larry Tuufuli, 24, entered the fray and his pistol was knocked from its holster and clattered to the floor. A bystander picked it up and returned it to him.

Young men ran about the auditorium shouting and punching officers.

The auditorium's steamy atmosphere was thick with flying cups, ice, metal folding chairs and other missiles.

Four persons fled the auditorium with handcuffs

Turn to Page 1-A, Col. 1

room for safekeeping, to be returned later to Tuufuli before anyone did something stupid with it.

But Metro officer Merwyn Lyons ended up on the wrong end of a flying piece of concrete tile that put a four-inch gash to his head and fractured his skull.

Still, some of the HPD cops were giving as good as they got. From my vantage point at the ring apron, I watched as two officers grabbed one of the Samoan grapplers and hit him across the top of his head with a billy club. The force of the blow split his head open to the point that his hair and scalp folded back almost over his ears. There was blood everywhere.

When the dust settled in the Civic and officers were able to restore order, the final tally included one new Hawaiian Heavyweight Champion, three skull fractures, nine arrests for assault and battery on a police officer, and countless other scrapes and bruises.

The next morning the fallen champ, Neff Maiava, came to me and asked if I had a key for handcuffs. Neff knew that we sometimes used cuffs as a handicapping gimmick in our matches. I found one of our universal handcuff keys, then asked Neff why he needed it. He admitted to me that one of his friends, after being arrested and cuffed during the

brawl the night before, managed to elude the police by hiding under a car in the parking lot, and was still in the cuffs.

Neff was smart enough to know they couldn't go ask the cops for a key. Should I help him, or turn the guy in? I was smart enough to know that a fan in jail was one less customer for our matches at the Civic.

I gave Neff the key.

Just how devoted were these fans?

I got a pretty fair indication when I was called in to the police station to answer some questions right after the riot. As I went up the steps of the station, I passed four big Samoan fans who were leaving. One of them had a big bandage on his head, and another had his arm in a sling.

One of the Samoans recognized me, and his face lit up. "Eh, Meestah Francis!" he shouted, a big grin spreading across his face. "What's happening nex' week at da Civic!?" ◆

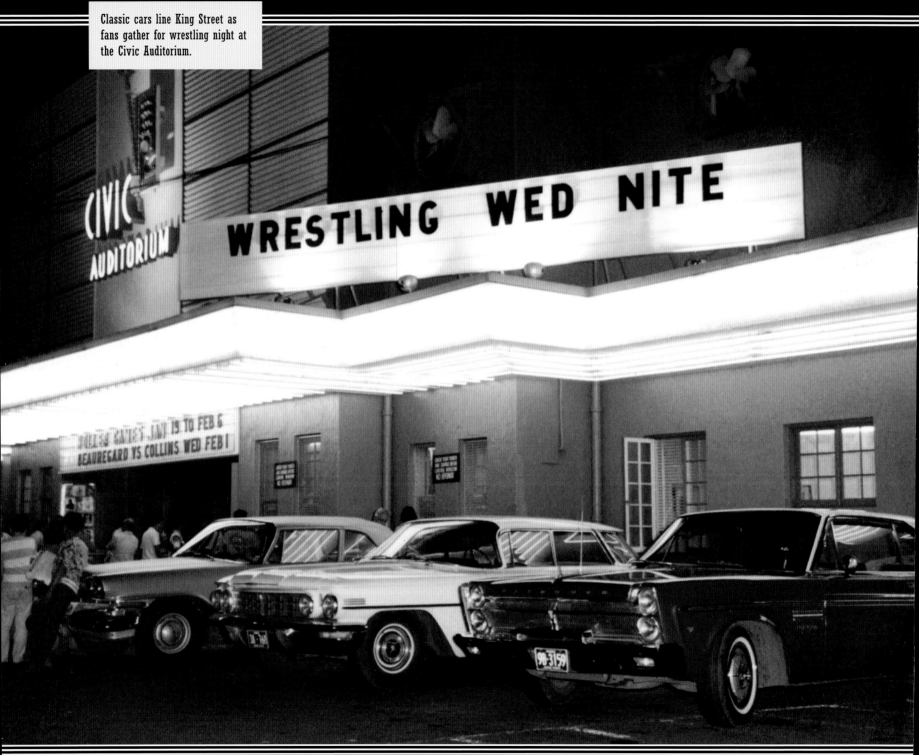

Classic cars line King Street as fans gather for wrestling night at the Civic Auditorium.

CIVIC AUDITORIUM

WRESTLING WED NITE

BEAUREGARD VS COLLINS WED FEB 1

CHAPTER 2

Playground in Paradise

I was a professional wrestler.

I had been living a gypsy's life for several years after World War II, crisscrossing the country and Canada to compete in an endless blur of wrestling matches, in every little town that had an arena, an auditorium or a gym.

Along the way I'd gained my share of notoriety. Stops in various wrestling territories had earned me several titles to go with my name. At different times in my career I was the Canadian Open Heavyweight Champ, the Texas Heavyweight Champ, the Pacific Northwest Heavyweight Champ, the Midwest Junior Heavyweight Champ and the World Junior Heavyweight Champ.

And I had all the attendant bumps and bruises, plus the thousands of miles on my car, to show for my labors.

Then, in 1955, I got a call from the local wrestling promoter in Hawaii, a fellow named Al Karasick, asking if I'd be interested in coming to wrestle in the Islands.

I could hardly believe my ears. Hawaii? Seriously? For a kid who grew up on the streets of Chicago during the Depression, Hawaii was the stuff of picture books and fantasies, just distant dreams. Did I want to come wrestle in Hawaii? It was the easiest question I'd ever had to answer in my life.

The moment I walked off the Pan American Airlines plane at the old airport in Honolulu, I knew I had truly arrived in paradise. The trade winds were blowing with that moist, tropical Island air, there was the scent of flower leis all around me and it struck me immediately that the folks who lived in this place were very lucky indeed. I had no idea at the time, of course, what was in store for me and my family: that I would one day be proud to call Hawaii my home.

Because I'd always been a history buff, I began getting a crash course in Hawaiian history. I wanted to soak up as much information as I possibly could about this magical place and its people. Maybe it was some kind of early omen, or maybe it was just a silly coincidence, but I was happily surprised to discover that I shared a birthday—June 11—with the most significant figure in all of Hawaiian history, King Kamehameha I. All I knew was, in exploring these beautiful Islands and beaches for my very first time, I truly felt like a king.

A little more browsing in the history books taught me that there was actually a rich and revered tradition of wrestling among the ancient Hawaiians. The powerful koa warriors (who were named after the koa-wood trees from which their weapons were crafted) trained in a deadly martial art called lua. The hand-to-hand-combat skill involved punching, kicking, wrestling, pressure-point attacks, bone breaking and strangulation. The koa warriors trained at night so no one else would learn their techniques.

9

Historical records say that King Kame-hameha, who was the greatest lua warrior of all, and his warriors knew as many as 300 moves that they used to dislocate or break opponents' bones without the use of weapons. By pressing on nerve centers, they could inflict severe pain on their enemies. They used high leaps and kicks in battle, and they oiled their bodies and cropped their hair short so they could slip out of their opponents' grasps.

Oh, those ancient Hawaiians knew how to wrestle.

For my first couple of weeks in Hawaii I was allowed to just relax, and was given a royal welcome. Al Karasick wanted to build up the upcoming match I had, so he showed me around town like a celebrity, taking me to the Honolulu Quarterback Club lunch to meet all the local media, like the great *Honolulu Advertiser* sportswriter Red McQueen. To my great good fortune, another of the guests at lunch that day was none other than The Yankee Clipper himself, New York baseball great Joe DiMaggio.

As I sat there, eating a most amazing, mouth-watering steak that they called teriyaki, in the company of Joltin' Joe himself in a true paradise called Hawaii, I had to pinch myself. Was this really happening?

I rented a little apartment on Liliuokalani Street in Waikiki, where I was surprised to find basketball great Wilt Chamberlain living in the apartment directly below mine. Wilt lived with a beautiful blonde girl, and played his bongo drums late into the evening. He was just a lanky, happy young kid then, enjoying Hawaii for a short time before going on to break every major NBA record in the books. Wilt had a relaxed charm that fit the Hawaii lifestyle—and apparently that same charm pleased the ladies, judging from his autobiography's claim that he bedded 20,000 women in his life.

As I strolled up and down Kalakaua Avenue in Waikiki, I looked up in wonder into the banyan trees at the Diamond Head end of Kalakaua, to find a handful of older Hawaiian men living in the trees, making coconut hats to sell to the tourists and enjoying their days playing cards and checkers on the beach. I certainly wasn't in Chicago anymore.

Prior to arriving in the Islands, I had, of course, expected what most Mainlanders envisioned: lazy, primitive conditions, thatched huts and naked hula girls in grass skirts. Some of those elements were still in evidence. When I went through Waimanalo then, I watched the local farmers still using oxen to work the taro fields.

But much of the Hawaii I found was also busy, growing, alive with energy. As I wandered around Waikiki—a big, burly haole with my hair then bleached blond by the sun—I was the proverbial fish out of water, the stuff of true culture shock among the local people. But they were very open and welcoming to me, and I loved every moment of my new playground.

I naturally gravitated toward the beach in Waikiki, where I ended up becoming close to and comfortable with all the beach boys, guys like Jesse Crawford and Coconut Willy. Their laid-back, "hang-loose" lifestyle and outlook helped me take the edge off, and not take myself or life too seriously.

Of course, even back then there was an unspoken "turf war" among the beach boys, guys like Rabbit Kekai, Turkey Love and Steamboat Mokuahi Sr., for their rightful share of the beach concessions.

Steamboat was the ruling alpha male of the beach boys. There was a continuous line of younger local guys, pretenders to Steamboat's throne, who wanted to muscle in on the beach concessions. That's when "hang loose" stopped and "my turf" took over.

As I was sitting on the beach at Waikiki one sunny afternoon, I heard some commotion a short distance down the beach. I looked to see Steamboat throwing punches at a kid much younger than he. The kid tried to escape Steamboat's barrage of blows, and the fight spilled from the beach out onto the middle of Kalakaua Avenue, stopping traffic.

The young kid was finally able to make his retreat, now much wiser about the rules of engagement on the beach. I never saw that kid back again.

But the fights were rare. Mostly, the beach boys had a huge appetite for fun. I saw it carried forward for years, even after I'd become a fixture in the Islands. One sunny afternoon years later, I was sitting with Duke Kahanamoku and Reverend Abraham Akaka at the Outrigger Canoe Club. We were all invited dignitaries for a law-enforcement convention, a gathering of many of the top police chiefs from around the country.

The beach boys—as always, up for anything—offered to take several of the stiff-collared Mainland police chiefs out for a canoe ride in the ocean off Waikiki. As they headed out, Duke smiled quietly and nudged me. "Watch this," Duke said with a little laugh. "Should be good."

The chiefs all got uncomfortably situated in their outrigger canoes, paddles in hand. They listened to the beach boys' instructions, and all tried gamely to follow them to the letter. They had no idea they were being set up.

With one fun-loving beach boy apiece in each of their canoes, offering to "steer," they were sitting ducks.

As we watched from the club, the little flotilla of police chiefs and beach boys worked its way well out into the surf offshore. Then, as if on cue, the beach boys all picked out one perfect wave, just the right size for their purposes.

On the beach boys' instructions, the police chiefs all paddled furiously to try to catch the wave. But behind them, each beach boy deftly angled his paddle into the water to capsize every canoe, sending all the chiefs splashing and sputtering into the sea. Some of these top cops couldn't

A syndicated newspaper column pays tribute to Gentleman Ed Francis' World Junior Heavyweight title in 1955.

swim, and the sight of their panicked faces as they were fished bodily out of the water and dragged back on board the canoes was a spectacle indeed.

Duke and I were roaring with laughter. He winked at me. "Told you," he said.

When I was still a malihini and it came time to do my work—what I'd been brought to paradise to do—I began by wrestling on the undercard in prelim matches at the historic Civic Auditorium on King Street.

I got a few victories under my belt, which set up a title bout for me in the Islands with Al Lolotai, who was a local favorite and the holder of *Ring* Magazine's sanctioned Hawaiian Champion Belt. I was definitely the "bad guy" in the title match, the guy the fans loved to hate, but I didn't mind.

Through what were no doubt some shady methods on my part, I managed to defeat Lolotai in

WRESTLING
TOMORROW
8 P.M.
CIVIC
AUDITORIUM
CHAMPIONSHIP
MATCH FOR
HAWAIIAN
TITLE
(2 out of 3 falls or
1 hr. 1 min. time limit)

AL LOLOTAI
(Champion)
Vs.

ED FRANCIS
(Challenger)
This is it! The match fans
have been clamoring for
has finally been signed up
by Promoter Al Karasick.
Lolotai will defend his Hawaiian championship and
Ring magazine gold belt
against the undefeated
"Gentleman" Ed Francis.
Under NWA rules, Francis's
world's junior heavyweight
title will not be at stake.
Don't miss this great match!

that title bout. I hung around for several Hawaiian matches to follow, my ears ringing week after week with the boos of the Island fans.

Eventually it was time to head back to the Mainland. But before I left Hawaii that first time, the promoter Al Karasick threw some hints my way that he might be looking to sell his rights for wrestling promotion in the Hawaii region. I stored that in the back of my mind as a wonderful pipe dream.

Then I bid my first aloha to the Islands and returned to the numbing Mainland cycle of road trips, cheap hotels and small-town wrestling matches that was my life.

On the Mainland once again, I was building a bigger and bigger name for myself on the wrestling circuit. I was proud that I was a "main-event guy" with a growing following and recognized skills in the ring.

But I couldn't deny that I began to hunger for something more. With my wife, Arlene, our family had grown to include four sons—Bill, Russ, Jim and Bob. Being an absentee father, always on the road and taking my lumps from town to town, was indeed getting old.

Still filed in the back of my mind were those hints I'd heard in Hawaii from promoter Al Karasick, that he might

be interested in selling the promotion rights for the wrestling business in the Islands. Of course, I'd never been a wrestling promoter before, but I figured there was a first time for everything. And honestly? The prospect of living and working in Hawaii was just too enticing not to pursue.

I called Karasick to find out if he was serious about selling his promotion rights. He told me he was ... for $10,000.

This stopped me cold. I certainly didn't have $10,000 in cash available in my pocket. It was 1961, and 10 grand was a king's ransom. Where could I get that kind of money?

Remember, salaries and incomes were very different then, in the 1950s and moving into the 1960s. Yes, I was making a living as a wrestler, but I was no millionaire movie star or banker. Even when I was the Junior Heavyweight Champion of the World, with a flashy belt to go with my title, in my best year I made $38,000 for the entire year. And I had to work very hard even to make that much, putting my body on the line night after night.

So the notion of just plopping down 10 grand—even if I had it—on an enterprise I knew could be risky? It was daunting, to say the least.

At the time, I was the Pacific Northwest Heavyweight Champion, working quite a bit in and around Oregon for a regional wrestling promoter there named Don Owen. I called Don and told him about the opportunity in Hawaii. Much to my surprise, Don agreed to lend me the $10,000 to pay Karasick.

It was a big gamble. I'd have to pay the money back to Don, and if the wrestling business didn't succeed in the Islands, then what? But I recall thinking, "Well, if you don't take a chance in life, you might miss it. You might miss out on something great."

Even though I hadn't actually done wrestling promotion in my career, I'd been around it for years. And I had one little bit of "insider's knowledge" up my sleeve that I hoped might pay big dividends in Hawaii. In many of the regions where I'd wrestled—the Pacific Northwest, New York, Chicago, Los Angeles and other places—there was local television coverage of wrestling. But I'd noticed when I was in Hawaii that Karasick's matches and his wrestling operation weren't on TV. I figured if I got over to Hawaii and could make a deal with a local TV station for a wrestling show, it could be a hit.

So, after some lengthy family discussions at home in the Francis household, I made the deal in Hawaii, packed up Arlene and the four boys, and off we went to our new Hawaiian adventure.

Initially, we rented a little one-bedroom apartment in Waikiki, on Liliuokalani Avenue, close to where I'd stayed when I visited Hawaii as a wrestler years earlier. There we were, the entire Francis family—all six of us, squeezed into that tiny apartment and falling all over each other in our cramped quarters.

But it was Hawaii, and it was wonderful.

In those first couple of days in our new paradise, the entire Francis family spilled out of the one-bedroom apartment to make a beach day of it in Waikiki. All four of my boys were young then, and they all loved the sand, the surf, the warm water. We all played water games, we built sand castles and we dug holes big enough to hide in. For my wife, Arlene, and me it was the perfect family day under the Hawaiian sun.

Until later that afternoon and evening, when we saw the toll that Hawaiian sun had taken.

It was the classic haole mistake: too much sun, not enough sunscreen. The entire Francis family dragged back to our one-bedroom, all burnt to cherry-red crisps. That night and in the days that followed, we had contests to see who wore the most blisters.

Hawaii Living Lesson No. 1: Sun hot. Shade good.

The Francis family's next stop was a rented house on the ocean side of Kalanianaole Highway, where I began in earnest to build the Hawaii wres-

tling promotion business that would occupy me for most of the next 20 years.

In time, from friends and insiders in Hawaii's wrestling business, I learned that Karasick had expected to take the $10,000 promotional-rights fee from me for his business, then hang around long enough to see me fail and resume his business as usual.

But I was determined not to let that happen. I was no stranger to hard work, and failure was not an option. Not when I had the warm Pacific lapping at my toes outside my door, a magnificent tropical playground for my family and the business opportunity of a lifetime.

In case anyone asked, I was planning to stay. ◆

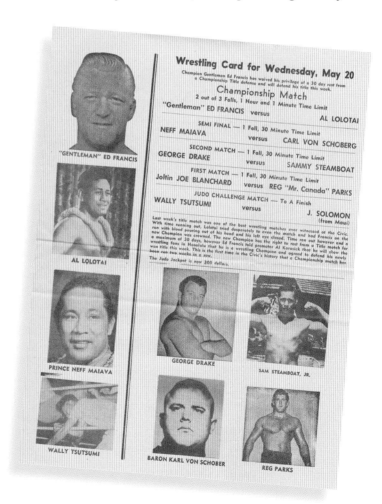

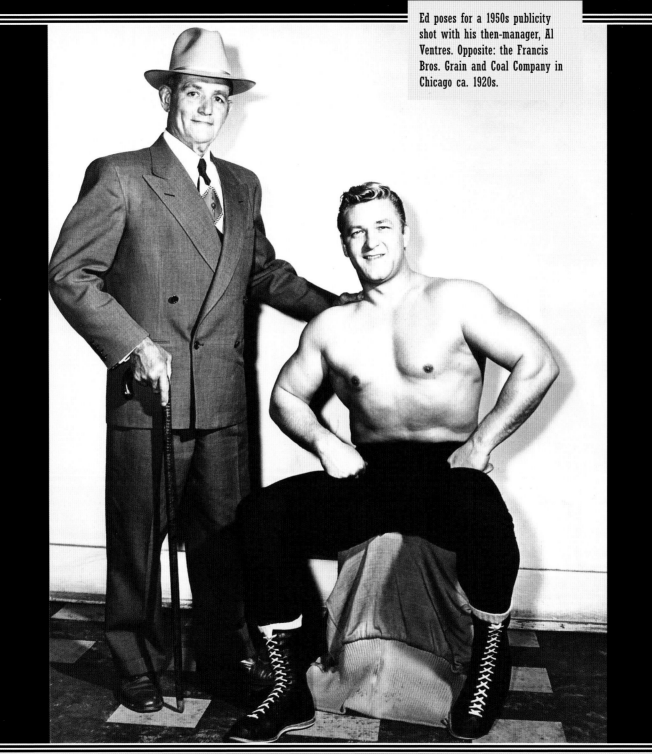

CHAPTER 3

The Kid from Chicago

Waking up every morning at our rented house on the beach in Hawaii—hearing the waves lapping onto the sand and feeling those gentle trade winds—was a far cry from my earliest upbringing in a tough, working-class neighborhood on the north side of Chicago.

Those Chicago streets were normally pretty tough, but that time in our country's history was the toughest of all. It was the early 1930s—The Great Depression.

My very earliest memory is that of sitting on my grandfather's lap when I was just a young boy. I recall him holding his ticking pocket watch up to my ear, feeding my fascination with all things from the distant past.

My grandfather Edmund Francis (thanks for letting me borrow your name, Grandpa) ran a coal and feed business, Francis & Sons, located on Chicago's High Street. He lent a gracious hand to everyone in the neighborhood—giving coal even to those who couldn't afford it, to heat their homes in the frigid winters, then looking the other way when the bills went out.

Then, my vivid memory of walking into our candlelit living room late at night, and staring dumbfounded at Grandpa as he lay in an open casket. He'd met his end oddly, on a hunting trip. During one cold night at the hunting lodge, he

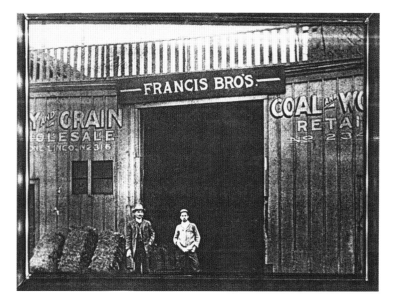

was burned by the asbestos bricks that served as foot-warmers. The burn turned gangrenous, but he refused to let the doctor remove his leg.

A procession of cars led by motorcycle cops led thousands to mourn at my grandfather's funeral. The grand, sad day was overlaid by the irony that the man who so many loved—the man who gave them heat to survive the winter—had himself fallen victim when he dodged the cold.

But at his passing, our family did what all families were doing in those hardscrabble days of the Depression—we pulled together, relied on each

15

THE KID FROM CHICAGO

other and carried on as best we could. Our neighborhood of people from all backgrounds—Germans, Jews, Poles, Italians—all co-existed, living in small, modest homes connected by cobblestone streets and alleys, scratching out a living, fighting for survival and finding joy in the smallest of things.

The streets in our neighborhood surrounding Fullerton Avenue in Chicago were still filled with horses in those earliest days, working alongside the cars. There were horse-drawn milk wagons and garbage wagons. A rag man would troll the alleys, and we would hear him shouting, "Rags and iron, rags and iron!" as he offered pennies for anyone's junk. On the hottest Chicago summer days, we kids would hitch a ride on top of the ice wagons, to scavenge chips of ice and try to defuse the blistering summer heat.

Every day on Fullerton Avenue was truly a variety show of fascinating neighborhood characters: World War I vets named Poompa, Yokes and Sponge-Nose Jerry, all hanging out on Fullerton at High near Pete Ballisini's ice cream shop. Yokes once sent me home with a quart of ice cream—a king's ransom for a young boy bringing the spoils home to his family. Not long after that, in the middle of a tough winter, Yokes was found frozen to death in a doorway near the Hollywood Theater.

Fritzy Dittman had a store in his home on Greenwood Avenue. He sold fish and oysters out of his basement. Tony the barber had a statue of Mussolini on his mantle. Tony also had a beautiful daughter who I made every attempt to visit. Tony's daughter once showed me something that I can never forget. "Look, watch this," she said, as she coaxed their family's cat to lap up some milk from a bowl. As the cat took in the milk, it started leaking, then pouring, out a hole in the side of the poor cat's neck. That hole had been chewed by a rat.

The rats. They were everywhere—in our homes, in the streets, clawing up from the sewers. For young boys like me and my brother, the rats became hunted prey. My brother and I "fished" for the rats in our backyard using a stick, a hook and some special bait we'd devised: braunschweiger mixed with shards of glass. Fortunately for the rats, those fishing expeditions proved unsuccessful.

As I walked to school one day, I spotted a rat sitting on the opposite side of a fence, with its tail dangling between the slats on my side. On impulse, I grabbed the tail and yanked. The rat flew off the fence and scampered away, and I was left holding the tail like a bloody kite string.

It was, of course, the adults who felt the hardships and ravages of The Depression most profoundly, as they watched their savings and their livelihoods slip away, and spent sleepless nights wondering how they'd make it through. But, for us kids, it was just the life we knew, and all that we knew.

The day started at 4 a.m., when I would stand in the charity line with my mother, waiting for hours along with hundreds of other families to get our handout rations of dried beans, cheese, cornmeal and lard. We'd fill our stomachs with lard sandwiches smothered in ketchup. Hardly fine dining, but it was better than the alternative—an achingly empty stomach.

Even worse in my recollection were the handout free shoes. They were glued together rather than sewn, and when the shoes heated up in the

Chicago summers, the glue would bubble and burn my feet. I took to cutting off the ends of the shoes to let the glue out and keep from getting blisters. Little did I know then that, with my improvised open-toed footwear, I'd crafted the Chicago version of the Hawaiian zori.

At night, my brother and I slept in the same single bed, head to foot. In the winter, we'd wake up to find ice on the walls, frozen over from the condensation of our breath during the night. Saturday was bath day. Mom would heat up the water on a double boiler in the kitchen. She'd fill up a tub, then we'd all take turns washing off the week's accumulation of dirt and sweat.

The day's motivating principle was simple then: How do I get what I want and manage to stay out of trouble? If I was hungry, I'd run past the vegetable stand, grab a potato and find a way to cook it over a fire in a vacant lot. To make a few pennies, I'd shine shoes in the local taverns for two cents a shine, or sell newspapers on the corner at a penny a sale. A fellow they called Radio Frank would pay me a penny to play my harmonica and dance the soft shoe.

Still, sometimes temptation got to be too much. Luxuries like candy and toys had an allure that turned me to a kid's short-lived life of crime. Back then we wore knickers, gathered at the knee with an elastic band. A strategically placed hole in my pocket would let me send stolen treats down the chute to land securely at the bottom of my pant leg. Quick fingers let me snatch candy when the shopkeeper wasn't looking, and I'd of course eat it before I got home. The perfect crime.

But my thieving days were numbered. For weeks I'd been "casing the joint" at F.W. Woolworth's, where a seemingly magical collection of lead toy soldiers had caught my

eye. In a fast-fingered flash, the entire army went marching into the trapdoor in my pocket and took safe bivouac in my pants. Home in my backyard, the soldiers and I played happily for hours.

We were engaged in a full-scale war together when my father got home and asked the inevitable: "Where'd you get those?" I first tried to sell the notion that I'd borrowed them from a friend, but my father could read my face for a liar's, and I admitted the truth.

Up I went by the scruff of my neck, carried back to Woolworth's with purloined army in hand. The return and an apology were not enough. My Dad ordered me to get down on the floor and kiss the manager's shoes. The manager felt bad for me, and said, "No, no, get up boy!" He must have thought my Dad was being too hard on me. But you know what? I never stole anything again.

Opposite: In the '20s the Francis family business delivered coal and feed supplies even to those who couldn't afford to pay. Right: Ed's 1944 merchant seaman certificate of identification.

Rumor had it that Dillinger's "lady in red," his double-crossing lover, lived for a time in an apartment behind our house on Fullerton Avenue. Then, one hot summer evening, as everyone sat on their porches sweltering from the heat, the word went out. My Dad had sent me across the street to the tavern to fetch him a bucket of beer. "Tell 'em not to put too much foam on it!" he instructed. I was 8 years old. I recall the buzz, the gossip spreading like wildfire down the hot Chicago street: "Dillinger's been shot!" "Melvin Purvis finally got his man!" Sure enough, Dillinger lay in a pool of his blood in the alleyway next to the Biograph Theater.

Years later, when I lived in Hawaii, I took my family to Chicago to see my old neighborhood, and we stopped by the Biograph Theater. A telephone pole was still standing, riddled with bullets from that night. My old home at 1452 W. Fullerton was gone—in its place, just a vacant lot.

Our family had had to vacate the Fullerton house—asked to do so by the tax man. With our home taken from us, we were forced to move to the Diversy Housing Projects with many other poor families. I was a teenager then, and quickly came to realize in that angry, dangerous environment that tougher was better. Bigger and stronger meant safer. Through some innate self-preservation instinct I began to steel myself, to gather strength for the long-distance obstacle race full of life challenges that lay ahead.

In those hard, corrupt Chicago days the "straight and narrow" was almost too narrow to find. As a teen in the city I became a target, a potential pawn for criminals and dirty cops alike. It was inevitable, then, that, one day, walking home from high school when I was 15, I would be drawn into the drama.

Of course, there were much bigger criminals than little-kid shoplifters roaming the streets of Chicago then. It was the era of real, brazen gangsters like Dion O'Banion and John Dillinger. O'Banion was ultimately taken out by Capone's men. I remember the clamor in our neighborhood on the day John Dillinger was taken down.

A guy stepped out of a car parked near our family's apartment and showed me a badge. "Get in the car," he said. There were two detectives in the car, and my heart was racing. I wondered what I'd done wrong. But the cop said he just wanted my help, and began showing me cards with criminals' pictures. I was in no position to argue, so I agreed to help, and promised to meet them that night at 8. "Don't tell anybody. Keep it under wraps," the cop warned.

I met them that night and they drove to the Little Sicily neighborhood in Chicago, a section of town with a distinct mafia influence. They also called the neighborhood "Little Hell" ... with good reason.

The cop explained the plan. He handed me a flask of booze and told me to swish some around in my mouth. Then he gave me some money and told me to walk into the saloon on the corner. There I was to buy a bottle of Jack Daniels, then meet them back at the car.

I did as asked, no problem. When I got back to the car, bottle of Jack in hand, the cop said, "Okay, I'm going to have to manhandle you a little now, but don't worry." He grabbed me by the collar, marched me back into the saloon and dragged me up to the bartender. "Did this man sell you whiskey?" he shouted, holding up my bottle. "Yes, he did," I said, then he hustled me back out of the saloon.

It wasn't hard to figure out that the cops wanted to nail the saloon for conspiracy to sell to a minor. So—job done? End of story? Not quite. My last task was to walk up the road and wait in the doorway of the Bowman Dairy garage. That's where I was to be picked up and taken home. But as I waited there, instead of a cop car pulling up, a big Lincoln Continental came screeching to a halt in front of me, and two different men jumped out. These were not cops.

One of the men wore a uniform, and told me he was part of the military's "suicide squad." The

two men pushed me into their Lincoln and headed back to the saloon, where they dragged me into a back room. They told me that the two cops were trying to shake down the bar owner for thousands of dollars, threatening to take him to jail for selling

'Gentleman Ed'

"GENTLEMAN ED" FRANCIS

to a minor. I was just a scared 15-year-old kid. I told the men how the cops had used me in their plan. But as I explained it all to them, the phone rang in the saloon ... and the call was for me!

It was the cop on the line, telling me to run out of the bar and he'd pick me up. Much easier said than done—I was surrounded in the saloon by a bunch of angry Italians, and the soldier from the suicide squad. Instead of obeying the cop, I told my captors what he'd said on the phone. The solider took pity on me, and asked where I lived. He took me to the streetcar and gave me money to get home, but not without a warning. He said, "Look in the newspaper tomorrow. There'll be a story about two dead cops found in an alley."

I went home. I didn't look in the newspaper the next day, and I never told my parents what happened.

For refuge from all the street toughs and neighborhood nastiness, I ended up finding my way to the Hamlin Park Fieldhouse. The big, cavernous gym was a gathering place for weightlifters, wrestlers and acrobats. For a teenage kid looking for an attachment and a diversion, it was like a free circus. The acrobats were hand-balancers who had their vaudeville stage act. I met a man named Lou Talibar, who took me under his wing as my first wrestling coach. He truly gave me my start in the career that would last a lifetime. I trained alongside Ruffy Silverstein, a great amateur champion from the University of Illinois.

But the performing spark was really ignited when I met the members of the German-American Weightlifting Club. These guys were tough, and they were jaw-droppingly strong. They taught me the one-armed bent press, and I learned to do it lifting my entire body weight. I had new role models, new goals, and I began touring with the club through German taverns all around Chicago, performing our feats of strength.

I'd never before known what it was like to play to an audience, to hear and feel their appreciation—and to maybe even get a little pocket money along the way. For me, this performing thing was new—and it was wonderful. I began to understand that it was

Ed learned the ropes of wrestling in the gyms and German taverns of Chicago.

all about the show: giving people a little something, however brief and marvelous, to take them away for an instant from our tough collective daily reality. Day by day, as I got stronger and bolder, a true performer and competitor was taking shape.

This new bug took me to a local carnival, where I would take on all comers in the ring. It was called an Athletic Show (or "At Show" as the carneys called it), and challengers were promised a dollar for every full minute they could survive in the ring against me. They were promised $100 if they could last 15 minutes.

There wasn't a truck driver, laborer or tough guy who made it past three minutes with me.

After a stint in the service in World War II as a merchant seaman with the Coast Guard, I somehow found my way back to the tough physical world of wrestling. My family, of course, never had the money to send me to college, so I felt like I didn't have the education to pursue other careers. And many of my strongest friendships and bonds had been formed with the athletes in those gyms and field houses in Chicago.

I returned there after the war, where I was lucky enough to meet the great Karl Pojello, a wrestling promoter who had been one of the finest wrestlers of his day. Pojello had been a true "shooter"—the term for a skilled wrestler who was not merely a "showman," but someone who could do some serious damage to you in the ring. A shooter—if he chose to—could put holds on you that would break your arm, break your leg or disable you. A shooter could pick you up in a suplex and slam you to the mat. A shooter could knock out an opponent.

Under Karl, I trained to be a fierce and feared shooter.

Pojello was managing some of the biggest names in wrestling: the world heavyweight champion, Jim "The Golden Greek" Londos, Maurice "The French Angel" Tillet and others. I began to studiously learn my craft under these greats. I learned

how to drop kick, how to hit the ropes and come off in a flying tackle, how to fall out of the ring without breaking my skull, and how to work with a different wrestler every night, sometimes five, six, seven nights a week.

I honed my skills as a shooter, and Pojello began booking me for matches around the country. Most followed the time-honored pattern of pitting a good guy—who we called a "baby face"—against a bad guy—who we called a "heel."

I became a heel. The guy the fans loved to hate. I wrestled hundreds upon hundreds of matches as the heel, making the fans crazy enough to riot. From Toronto to Tallahassee, Green Bay to Galveston, New York to New Mexico and all points in between, wherever the name "Gentleman" Ed Francis appeared on the card, I tried to make sure the fans got their money's worth.

I enjoyed great success as a competitor. At various times in my active career, I held the titles of World Junior Heavyweight Champion, Canadian Open Heavyweight Champion, Hawaiian Heavyweight Champion, Pacific Northwest Heavyweight Champion and the Texas Heavyweight Champion.

It was a tough way to make a living, full of knocks and bruises and endless nights on the road. But it was also a show that got fans out of their seats and on their feet, screaming with excitement at every "high spot" in the matches. It was terrific entertainment, and it was a business.

I learned the business of wrestling well, from the ground up. ◆

Curtis Iaukea flies across the ring at the Civic Auditorium.

CHAPTER 4

Making It Up As We Go

What had I gotten myself and my family into?

Sitting with my wife, Arlene, and our four boys in our tiny rented one-bedroom apartment on Liliuokalani Avenue in Waikiki, I had to wonder.

Yes, Hawaii was a wonderful paradise. No argument there.

But this was no longer a vacation. I had mouths to feed, rent to pay—and a $10,000 debt hanging over my head. In 1961, 10 grand was no small sum. It was like an enormous boulder threatening to roll down off the Pali and crush me.

To get our infant business off and running, I began to gather and enlist whatever solid local wrestling talent I could find at arm's reach in Hawaii. Among the names in our earliest going in 1961 were all the local boys: Sammy Steamboat, Neff Maiava, Al Lolotai, Lucky Simonovich and a few others.

There was also some available wrestling talent that already had a history of wrestling in the Islands: Billy White Wolf, Luigi Macera, Lou "Shoulders" Newman, King Curtis, Bob Shibuya, Stan Kowalski, Hard-Boiled Haggerty and several others.

Our first couple of weeks of matches at the Civic Auditorium did little to ease my fears. The historic old Civic had a seating capacity of somewhere north of 5,500—but, in our first two weeks, we got 800 people one week and 600 the next.

Francis To Promote

Al Karasick, who promoted professional wrestling at the Civic Auditorium for 26 years, has sold his territorial rights to Edmund Francis, it was learned yesterday.

It was also reported that Karasick will remain as the National Wrestling Alliance representative in the State of Hawaii and other Pacific areas.

RECENTLY, HE announced plans of extending his wrestling operations to The Philippines, Hong Kong, Japan and other areas. Most of his operations, however, will be confined to booking wrestlers and arranging matches for them in these areas.

Karasick left for the Mainland Tuesday night to attend ceremonies in Cincinnati, Ohio, at which time his son, Joseph, will be ordained as a rabbi. He expects to return here in early July.

Before leaving he said Francis will promote wrestling at the Civic Auditorium. He pointed out that Francis, recognized by the NWA as its junior heavyweight champion, has had wide experience in professional wrestling and has traveled all over the world.

Francis and his wife arrived here several weeks ago with their four sons, who have been placed in a local school.

IT WAS reported that

Francis bought out Karasick's promotional rights because of a desire to settle down.

"Francis has many friends and good connections in professional wrest-

ED FRANCIS

I started to sweat. And I never stopped.

I knew it wasn't that this was an "unknown," a brand-new commodity that was completely unfamiliar to audiences in Hawaii. After all, the man from whom I bought the Hawaii regional wrestling-promotion rights, Al Karasick, had been staging and promoting professional wrestling in the Islands for a full 25 years at that point, since 1936.

Karasick's business saw its heyday in Hawaii during World War II and shortly thereafter, when Oahu teemed with military personnel, many of whom proved to be avid wrestling fans.

Then Karasick's matches for decades became a solid mixture of local stars with faces visiting

23

from the Mainland and Japan. Among the wrestlers Karasick brought in and promoted in Hawaii was a big star from Japan named Rikidozan, who would go on to ultimately become the true "kingpin" promoter for many years of the flourishing wrestling business in Japan.

I had seen firsthand, when I myself wrestled for Karasick a few years earlier in Hawaii, that the business in the Islands had the potential of being a true crossroads for big-name wrestlers going from the U.S. mainland to Asia and Australia and back. That's why I chose to name my new wrestling business Mid-Pacific Promotions, to reflect our position at the geographic center of these distinct wrestling regions.

It also wasn't that Honolulu's wrestling venue, the Civic Auditorium, at 1314 S. King St., was unfamiliar to the local crowds. It had been built way back in 1933. Beyond housing Karasick's wrestling matches, the venerated old arena had played host to countless boxing matches, sumo matches, roller derbies and music acts of all kinds.

Legendary rock 'n' roll acts took the stage at the old Civic in Honolulu beginning in the '50s and forward, names like Jerry Lee Lewis, Frankie Avalon and Chubby Checker. Ritchie Valens played the Civic in 1958, in a giant "Show of Stars" that also featured Buddy Holly and the Crickets, Paul Anka and many more rock stars.

The promoter of those music events, along with the boxing matches and so many other shows at the Civic, was an amazing fellow named Ralph Yempuku. Yempuku ran his Boxing Enterprises operation out of the offices at the Civic, so when I moved into those offices with my brand-new Mid-Pacific Promotions, he and I became officemates. But to Yempuku I was just the "new kid on the block." I sensed from the start that Yempuku, like so many others, figured I wouldn't be around for long.

Remember, my predecessor, Al Karasick, had been handling all the wrestling in Hawaii for a quarter-century. He was the man Yempuku had known and worked with. All they knew about me was that I was a wrestler from the Mainland. Who was I to come invade their space at the old Civic?

(I remembered what I'd heard from friends in wrestling circles that Karasick himself had expected me to fail. He'd figured that I would pay him his $10,000 rights fee, give the promotion a try in the Islands and lose my shirt, then tuck my tail and leave, allowing him to move right back in and pick up where he'd left off, just $10,000 richer.)

Every day in those first few months at the Civic, I'd come to work and pass Ralph Yempuku, who was sitting at his desk reading *The Honolulu Advertiser.*

"Morning, Ralph!" I'd say in my most chipper, convivial voice.

"Mmmm," Ralph would half-grunt, barely looking up from his paper to acknowledge me.

Since we shared so few words, I knew little about this man with whom I shared office space. But in time I found out some remarkable things.

Yempuku was born on a plantation on the Big Island and moved to Kahuku when he was a kid. After McKinley High and UH, Yempuku volunteered with the Territorial Guard when World War II broke out. But after Pearl Harbor, Yempuku and his fellow nisei guard members were classified "enemy aliens."

Yempuku was first and foremost an American. So, rather than backing down, he led a group of other Japanese-Americans like himself, who volunteered for duty at Schofield Barracks. Then Yempuku volunteered for the Army's Office of Strategic Services, and became a member of the "Merrill's Marauders."

As part of that team for the U.S. war effort, Colonel Yempuku and his men parachuted behind enemy lines in Burma to destroy Japanese supply lines and communications. His team later parachuted onto Hainan Island to liberate Australian and Dutch prisoners of war.

So my new officemate, the man behind the newspaper across from me at the Civic every day, was one courageous fellow and a true war hero. But I was thinking about other things. I had the next week's wrestling card to plan.

C-6 THE SUNDAY ADVERTISER   July 16, 1961

Promoter Ed Francis is shown with wife Arlene and sons Russ, Bob, Jim and Bill.

Val Valentine

Promoter Is Family Man

Ed Francis, Honolulu's new wrestling promoter, is a family man.

Father of four sons, Francis has established residence in Honolulu and with his wife, Arlene, has gone into business under Mid-Pacific Promotions.

He bought out long - time friend Al Karasick's wrestling promotional rights at the Civic Auditorium in April because he wanted to settle down for the kids' sake.

"I FIRST came to Honolulu in 1958 to wrestle for Al and I fell in love with the place," said Francis. "So when I had chance to buy Al's business, ▢▢ped at the chance and I maintain his high

▢▢'s four sons ▢ Russ 8 and ▢l active in ▢ Athletic

Club and attend Koko Head School.

Francis is coaching the Tee-Ball team on which his two youngest sons play.

Mrs. Francis is also athletic minded and does a lot of swimming and tennis.

Francis, who celebrated his 35th birthday on Kamehameha Day, started wrestling at the age of 12 in the Chicago Park district. As a pro he was trained by Lou Talabar and managed by Ed "Strangler" Lewis.

RATED FOR many years as one of the top junior heavyweights in wrestling, Francis has held the Hawaiian, Texas and other state championships. He won the world's junior heavyweight belt, which he held for several years, until he retired undefeated.

Since taking over as pro-

moter here Francis has kept up his wrestling, occasionally climbing into the ring to keep in shape.

Sons Bill, Russ and Jim all aspire to become wrestlers and follow in their father's footsteps. Bob hasn't quite made up his mind.

With his sons and wife at ringside, Francis isn't lacking support when he does climb into the ring as a wrestler and not as a promoter to iron out differences.

I would not go quietly. I was certainly not afraid of hard work, and I'd spent the better part of my early life hearing people tell me what I couldn't do. When others around me in Depression-era Chicago were begging for handouts, I was shining shoes and doing odd jobs.

Then, when I found my way to the gym and started building my strength, my father said to me, "You shouldn't be lifting weights. You're going to rupture yourself." But it was the weight lifting that made me the star of the German American Weight-lifting Club, performing my one-armed bent press in taverns to the applause of all the beer drinkers.

Now, if anyone chose to make it tough for me to succeed in Hawaii? I could do tough.

Of course, I recognized from the beginning that I had an uphill battle on my hands. I was hardly the first former wrestler who tried to turn his fortunes toward promoting wrestling. There had already been a long and blemished history of veteran wrestlers in territories all across the U.S. who set their sights on becoming wrestling promoters, only to meet with dismal failure.

The reality, of course, is that the skill sets of wrestlers and promoters are markedly different. The best wrestlers are athletes and showmen, eager to be on display and in the spotlight. The best promoters are schemers, visionaries, willing to work tirelessly behind the scenes and always focused on marketing the product. In the show business that is professional wrestling, wrestlers are the show. Promoters are the business.

So it was no surprise to me, when we brought wrestlers in from the Mainland, that many of them told me the same thing: "Hey, Ed, the Mainland guys think you're gonna fall on your face here. They all say you're a wrestler, not a promoter. What do you know about the business side?" Of course, the more I heard of others' doubts about our operation, the more determined I was to succeed.

One of the things I was lucky enough to figure out in the very earliest going as we staged our matches in Hawaii was: First and foremost, you have to know your audience. You have to know their culture, their value set, their likes and dislikes. After travelling the country and working in the Northeast, the Midwest, the Northwest and the deep South, it was easy for me to see that Hawaii was unique, like no other place in the country or on the planet.

Who was our audience? Filipinos and Japanese, Hawaiians and Samoans, Chinese, Koreans, haoles and every possible blend in between. The characters in our matches had to key on these cultural differences among people, understand what made them tick and recognize their preexisting feelings. If I was to succeed at all in Hawaii—and, believe me, I was, because I had a family to feed—I was going to literally play to the hometown crowd.

To do that for the best possible result, I became its student.

As each match played itself out for the fans in Hawaii, I found a spot in the arena from where I could watch and listen. I studied the fans' faces, the noises they made, when they'd jump out of their seats or when they seemed the least bit disinterested.

For our "product" in the ring, I became like the guy you see administering the soft-drink taste tests on TV. Try this, then try this. Which do you like better? Which would you buy?

I'd make sure and position myself near an exit at the end of the matches. That way I could hear what people were saying as they were walking out.

Curtis Iaukea takes on Jim Hady in a tag team match under the watchful eye of veteran referee Wally Tsutsumi. Opposite: a Wednesday night wrestling card at the Civic.

"Ho, you ba-lieve what wen' happen?"
"No way I t'ought da guy was goeen' win!"
"He gotta come back nex' week, get his revenge, eh!"

By harvesting this "market research," this real-life, real-timc fccdback about our wrestlers, I became more adept at changing up the dramas, turning the formula on its ear and twisting the dynamic between opponents for the biggest fan reaction.

Beyond that, I still believed I had an ace in the hole—if I could just extract it.

Part of the dream I brought with me to Hawaii was the hope of bringing pro wrestling to the television audience in the Islands. I'd travelled enough on the Mainland to see that it could be a key component of wrestling's success in other markets. Despite the long tradition of wrestling that Karasick had laid in Hawaii, there was no real precedent for TV coverage there.

So, if I could just get us on TV …

I made the rounds to all the TV stations in Honolulu, doing the very best sales pitch I could. Initially, no one was taking the bait. It was too expensive, it was too complicated, it was too limited in audience appeal—all the TV guys had a reason it couldn't or shouldn't be done.

I had one last hope: a meeting with a fellow named Dan Kawakami, the program director of the then-ABC affiliate in Honolulu, KHVH-TV, part of the Kaiser Broadcasting empire. I swallowed hard and stepped into Dan's office.

Dan began by throwing at me the same resistance I'd been hearing all around town. Too difficult. Too costly. Who'd want to watch it?

Then Dan threw yet another roadblock in the mix. "Besides, Mr. Francis," Dan said to me, "everybody knows wrestling is all phony."

I took one quick second to process his concern. Now what? Was I going to let this one last shot at TV slip away? No.

27

"Mr. Kawakami," I said after a moment. "When you run the TV commercials on your station for Tide detergent or Colgate toothpaste, they always say 'new and improved,' don't they?"

"I ... I suppose they do," Kawakami said. I could tell he was puzzled now.

"And, do you think they're really 'new and improved?' Or is it just a marketing ploy, to sell more of the same old soap and toothpaste?"

Kawakami had to concede: He doubted there was much new or improved in the worlds of Tide and Colgate.

I pressed on. "But people are still buying the product, aren't they? So ... true or not ... it's really all about the marketing, the presentation?"

Kawakami had to grant me that. The heart of the sale is the marketing.

"My product is no different," I said to him. "I'm going to give your audience a wrestling show like they've never seen before. New and improved!"

We both smiled. There was a long pause in Kawakami's office. To me, it felt like an eternity.

"All right, listen," Kawakami said at last. "Thirteen weeks. I'll give you that, and we'll see how it goes."

I fairly floated out of his office and into the Honolulu sunshine. I had a contract for a TV wrestling show in Hawaii. It was one enormous step closer to realizing the dream I'd had before I left Oregon, before I'd taken the risk of borrowing $10,000, before I'd moved my family lock, stock and barrel across an ocean.

Only one small problem now. I had no idea how to produce a TV show.

Part of the agreed-upon deal with Kawakami was to bring our wrestlers into his KHVH studios to compete. This, in theory, would keep the costs down, avoiding the more expensive "on-location" remote coverage that would require dragging cameras and production equipment out to the Civic.

Fine for Kawakami and his bottom line, but now the onus was on me to create a suitable wrestling environment inside his station. What was already there for me was … nothing. An empty room with lights and cameras, nothing more.

First order of business: a wrestling ring.

I surveyed the space at KHVH, and quickly realized that the ring would need to be smaller than what we were used to, and shorter because of the low ceiling in the studio. Not ideal, but it was what it was.

I needed help, and help came in the form of one true Godsend: a man named Nolan Rodrigues, who had been a fixture connected with Karasick's wrestling operation.

Nolan knew everyone in Honolulu, and he and his friends were "can-do" guys who could get anything done. I didn't know it in the earliest going, but Nolan would become a lifelong friend and facilitator for me, a man I'd rely on to make the impossible happen time and again, a man who my own kids would come to call Uncle Nolan.

Nolan would go on to referee many of our biggest matches, he would be our construction engineer on countless projects and, above all, he would be a good and close friend. But, first, he needed to build me a wrestling ring.

No problem. Nolan set to the task in the backyard of a friend's house, building it there before transporting it in pieces to KHVH. Nolan and his crew collected parts from junk yards around Oahu, and began to erect the ring to the specs we'd calculated.

Since the allotted space in the studio was smaller than would house a real ring, we had to improvise. No room for standard, full-size wrestling-ring posts, so Nolan cut them down to size. Then we attached the ropes to the smaller posts … and the whole ring caved in. So Nolan welded together piping and flanges instead of the standard chains to hold the entire contraption together.

Somehow, in our limited time frame, Nolan pulled it off and we had ourselves a ring. I'd heard tales in Hawaii of the menehunes, cheerful, mythical little men of superhuman strength who could miraculously build great stone walls and other edifices literally overnight. Well, Nolan Rodrigues wasn't a menehune, but …

The Rodrigues Ring we dragged into the KHVH studios wasn't quite as strong as a regulation wrestling ring. We knew that the big men who'd be flinging themselves around in it would need to be careful. They'd have to pull their punches, treat the ropes with kid gloves. Otherwise, Uncle Nolan's Great Achievement might come crashing down on live TV in a tangled heap, revealing its true colors as a kapakahi pile of scrap metal and random parts.

That would be bad. So, we would be careful. Or I'd kill somebody.

Next item on the "Ed Francis Televised Wrestling to-Do List": TV commentators.

Just like the wrestling shows I'd seen on the Mainland, I knew there needed to be someone to narrate the shows, to bring all the action to the fans watching at home. I was more than willing to try to help out on that side, but I wasn't foolish enough to think I could handle the chores all by myself.

That's when some of my wrestlers—local-boy Sam Steamboat, wrestling legend Lou Thesz and others—told me about a guy they thought might be  a great fit for our young operation. He, too, was a wrestler, they said, and he had a history of competing over the past several years in the Islands. They told me he was bright, affable, quick with a phrase. He was a guy who, in their estimation, could be a solid contributor as a face and voice for our televised shows.

His name: James "Lord Tally Ho" Blears. ◆

Lord Tally Ho Blears wore many hats for 50th State Big Time Wrestling, including announcer, referee (below) and wrestler (signing autographs, opposite).

CHAPTER 5

Tally Ho!

At my earliest meetings with this fellow named James "Lord Tally Ho" Blears, I took to him immediately.

Who wouldn't? If you look up the definition of "likeable" in the dictionary, Lord Blears' picture is there. Blears had a big smile, a warm handshake and a million stories. But, far more than that, he was the perfect combination of ingredients to help our Mid-Pacific Promotions operation.

Number one: He knew Hawaii. Blears had wrestled there himself over the past several years, so he knew the people, the culture, the local sensibilities. Even though he had that amusing "uptown" British accent, his temperament and affability felt very comfortably at home in the Island environment. He was somehow a man from a faraway land who still felt like "da kine."

Number two: He knew wrestlers. Lord Blears had spent many years after World War II much as I had, traveling the mainland U.S. and taking the ring with opponents of all shapes, sizes and backgrounds. Blears could step effortlessly into the important, added role of booker of many of our top acts in the years ahead. By combining his huge list of wrestling contacts with mine, we had most of the Mainland and Asia covered. No matter who we wanted to invite to wrestle for us in the Islands, either I knew somebody or Blears knew somebody,

who knew somebody, so we could get it done.

Number three: He knew TV. Blears had plenty of exposure to televised wrestling coverage in Los Angeles, around the likes of "Gorgeous George," Freddie Blassie and the legendary Lou Thesz, for promoter and L.A. Olympic Auditorium owner Aileen Eaton. Blears was a smart, quick-witted speaker, able to think on his feet and be comfortable in front of the TV cameras.

For all these reasons, I recognized that Blears could be an enormous asset to our operation. In short order, Blears and I became business partners in every aspect of the operation.

When Blears first came in as part of Mid-Pacific Promotions, it was like instant family. He'd brought his wife and kids with him, and they took an apartment right on the beach in Waikiki, by the Moana Hotel. When I'd go by to see Blears, often with my kids, everyone would play on the sand and in the surf of Waikiki. It was a wonderful "backyard playground" to have, and our two families merged and bonded.

Blears and I began planning matches every week, and shaping what would be the maiden voyage of our TV wrestling show on KHVH. We depended completely on each other. We had to. There was no one else. Blears and I were the wrestling bookers, the travel coordinators, the TV-show producers, the accountants and the go-fers to make the airport, hotel, food and production runs. There were no assistants. It was us.

Blears and I would face off in the office at the Civic every day and do whatever it took. I'd dictate letters to wrestlers and their representatives with our offers to come to Hawaii, and Blears would type them furiously with just two of his fat fingers pounding the keys. He did the letter typing, because I couldn't spell worth a damn. Still can't.

Probably too often, whenever there was a hole in one of our upcoming wrestling cards, either Blears or myself would fill the hole, going back into the ring ourselves on a Wednesday night at the Civic. In every conceivable way, Mid-Pacific Promotions became a two-man operation 24/7.

There was one rare occasion when Blears and I even squared off in the ring against each other for Hawaii fans. One particular week, a match had fallen through on our card on short notice, so Blears and I agreed to wrestle a "clean match" against one another.

A clean match is when two "baby faces"—in ring parlance, two good guys—wrestle each other. But around 15 minutes into our scheduled 20-minute match, things took a turn for the worse. Blears had a headlock on me, and I threw

him hard into the ropes. He came flying back off the ropes and hit me with a flying tackle. I jumped up and put my right knee forward.

With all of his momentum moving forward at me, Blears' face slammed into my knee. I inadvertently caught my business partner right across the bridge of his nose, and I could feel and hear the cartilage compress against my knee with a crunch.

Instantly, blood spilled from Blears' nose and splashed across the mat. There was no stopping it. We both tried to conceal the surprised looks on our faces—this wasn't the way the match was supposed to go at all. Lord held his broken nose in his hands, but the blood kept flowing.

The referee did the only thing he could do: He stopped the match. Blears and I shook hands in the ring to demonstrate to the fans that there were no hard feelings, then we hurried Blears to the hospital to try to get that big nose of his set straight on his face.

A few days later, with Blears' face still taped to help his nose heal, we spoke about the match. I suggested that it was probably best if we didn't wrestle each other again. Blears didn't disagree.

Lord Blears felt about our young business exactly as I did: that we couldn't stand still, just promoting the same Wednesday-night matches week in and week out, without growing and expanding. We wanted to take our product to more audiences in Hawaii, to give our wrestlers more paychecks and, of course, to bring in more revenue.

So Blears and I began staging matches for fans on the outer islands, first on the Big Island and Maui, then on Kauai. The fans there had, of course, been able to get a taste of our wild brand of entertainment by watching our weekly show on KHVH-TV. That meant when Blears and I and a handful of stars rolled into the venues in Kona or Hilo, Kahului or Lihue, there was already in place a hungry, eager audience.

We also found our way to two more venues in which our wrestlers could compete: Conroy Bowl at Schofield Barracks, and Bloch Arena at Pearl Harbor. Many of the military guys and their families on the bases had gotten a taste for pro wrestling in or around their hometowns on the Mainland, and they were terrific fans for us as well.

The Civic and the outer islands, Schofield and Pearl—for Blears and me, our "dance cards" were getting unbelievably full. It was without question the "careful-what-you-wish-for" syndrome: We were thrilled with the fan response, but we were juggling as fast as we could to keep all our Mid-Pacific Promotions balls in the air.

Still another addition to our duties was an idea from Lord Blears: He suggested we put out a magazine promoting our matches and our wrestlers. It sounded like a great idea, but neither of us had ever published a magazine before.

That didn't stop Blears. Somehow, he pulled it all together, getting ads sold in the thing and filling it with articles about every aspect of our wrestling operation. If you looked in the magazine, you'd see the names of all kinds of writers who wrote the articles. But, in truth? Blears made up all the names. He wrote 90 percent or more of the magazine articles himself.

One of the easiest parts of our job was getting wrestlers to come to the Islands. In most cases, whenever they got our call, or the letter that was hand-pecked by Lord Blears on our typewriter, I'm sure they felt much as I did the first time I was invited to wrestle in Hawaii. Seriously? No need for arm-twisting.

The deal was simple: For most, we'd pay airfare, a hotel for a week and $150 per week guarantee. Beyond that, they were on their own. If they were bigger stars, main-event guys, we'd offer them a higher weekly guarantee. It was a sliding scale, based on their star power. The top fan favorites, guys like Curtis "The Bull" Iaukea or "Handsome" Johnny Barend, or a world champion like Lou Thesz, would get the bigger money.

Blears and I tried to make sure our guys were

happy. For me, maybe it was some kind of holdover from my days during the Depression, when we all needed to help each other and gave to whoever had nothing. I tried to pay my wrestlers a little extra—ideally, more than they were accustomed to getting on the Mainland and elsewhere—just to earn their loyalty and good attitude.

Both Lord Blears and I knew what it felt like as a wrestler, when you thought the promoter was "lowballing" you, undervaluing you,

making you put your body on the line while keeping the lion's share of the profits himself. I wasn't about to be "that guy," and neither was Blears.

Tally Ho Blears takes on Hans Mortier at the Civic Auditorium.

For any of our wrestlers, I'd always try to ask myself, "If I was in their position, what would I think I was worth?" It was of paramount importance to us that our wrestlers, the guys who truly were the show, felt as though they were being dealt a fair deal.

In one single instance, a Japanese wrestler who we'd brought in for one of our cards came

James Blears spent the years after World War II traveling the wrestling circuit throughout the U.S.

to me and complained that he wasn't being paid enough. He was no big star, but I guess he thought he was.

I thought about it for a minute, then I said to him, "I'll tell you what. Why don't you go get your accountant, then come back in here and I'll open my books to you. You and your guy can look over my books, see what you're getting paid, see what other guys are getting paid and see how much I make on the matches. My books are wide open to you. So let me know when you'd like to schedule that."

I never heard from him again on the subject of money. He didn't wrestle for us in the Islands for long.

With Blears and I as their "hosts," all the wrestlers enjoyed their time in the Islands. For most, it was the first time they'd been to Hawaii and, of course, with the beaches and all the natural beauty, it was a feast for the senses.

But even more than that, Hawaii gave the wrestlers a luxury they didn't get to enjoy on the Mainland: They could stay in one hotel or apartment for a series of wrestling dates.

On the Mainland, the wrestlers' rhythm was to get up, drive a couple of hundred miles to an arena, compete, then drive back home another couple of hundred miles. Life on the road was an endless succession of cars, buses and travel. In Hawaii, it was a quick trip over to the Civic, or just to the outer islands or the military bases, and the luxury of spending time in one central place, living and working in paradise. Blears and I saw every day that our wrestlers loved the Islands. Most of them never wanted to leave.

Blears himself loved the Islands like nobody else. He had grown up as an expert swimmer, so in Hawaii it was only natural that he developed a love of surfing. It became his huge lifelong passion, one that he would pass along to his kids. Surfing kept Blears in shape, it kept him tanned a golden brown and, on too many days, it kept him out of the office.

I didn't begrudge Lord his love for surfing. I loved the beaches and the ocean in Hawaii as well, so I understood. But there were many days that I found myself once again pacing the floor of the offices in the Civic as Ralph Yempuku peered over his paper to watch me going back and forth, worrying about next week's matches, while Blears was out enjoying a south swell.

Blears' "in the office one day, surf the next" lifestyle made it all the more critical that, when he and I were together, we focused laserlike on the needs of the business. We didn't take a lot of time to talk about other things.

As astonishing as it seems, maybe that's why, in the almost 20 years that I ended up working shoulder-to-shoulder with Blears promoting wrestling in Hawaii, he never said one word to me about his World War II experiences. I only learned much later about what he had endured in the war years. It is a truly remarkable tale.

Blears was just 17 years old at the start of World War II. He was already a great competitive swimmer, but he was too young in his native England to enter the Royal Navy. The merchant marine needed radio officers, and Blears' knowledge of Morse code helped him wrangle his way in.

Blears found his way to an assignment on a Dutch merchant ship named the *Tjisalak*, because it needed an English radio officer. He served ably on board through the war until March 26, 1944, when, in the middle of the Indian Ocean, two torpedoes from a Japanese submarine slammed into the hull of the *Tjisalak* and sank it.

Blears was by then 21. He was among the ship's 77 crewmen and 27 passengers who were taken aboard the sub as prisoners by the Japanese.

But the Japanese had no intention of holding on to their prisoners. They had other plans: the wholesale slaughter of every one of their captives.

One by one, the Japanese would hit each of the men, then drag him up to the front of the sub. There, amid choruses of laughter from the Japanese crew, a swordsman would decapitate the prisoner, slicing off his head with a single broad blow and dumping his lifeless body overboard.

As the carnage on the foredeck continued, other captives were tied in pairs and marched behind the conning tower, to meet their end by way of a gunshot to the head by other Japanese soldiers.

Blears, like all of his shipmates, knew it was just a matter of time—and not much time—until it was his turn. Blears was struck by a Japanese soldier with the flat of his sword, then tied, with his wrists behind him, to one of the other prisoners, a man named Peter Bronger.

Now Blears' survival instinct kicked in, and it was a powerful one.

When he was being tied, Blears made certain he kept his wrists as far apart as he could. That way, Blears reasoned, once the Japanese soldier finished tying him, Blears could still get a hand free.

Two Japanese officers then approached Blears and Bronger. They were wielding a sword and a sledgehammer. At the last moment, Blears kicked at them with his foot and pulled a hand free from the ropes behind him.

In one swift, desperate move, dragging his shipmate Bronger with him, Blears dived off the sub into the icy waters of the Indian Ocean.

Down Blears went, deeper and deeper into the water. He could see and hear machine-gun bullets from above as they pierced the water all around him.

Blears surfaced for an instant to gasp for air, then dove again. Still the hail of machine-gun bullets came. Blears surfaced and dove again and again until the sub had drifted a distance away, and the shooting stopped.

Somehow, miraculously, Blears had not been hit. He was alive.

Blears' ease in front of the television cameras was just one of the traits he brought to Mid-Pacific Promotions. Left: Keeping the peace during a ringside altercation at the Honolulu International Center Arena. Opposite: Blears calls a match using Mid-Pacific Promotions' state-of-the-art ringside audio-visual equipment.

Blears looked to the man he was still tethered to, Bronger. He was dead. It looked as though he'd been killed by a sword blow, and Blears suspected Bronger had died before they ever hit the water together.

Now Blears figured his own—and

perhaps his only—chance for survival was to swim back to his sinking ship, the *Tjisalak*. Perhaps he would find food, water, a radio or even a lifeboat. Blears worked himself free from Bronger, bid him a respectful farewell and began to swim. His life depended on it.

Blears had been a champion swimmer in school, and had even been training for a spot on the English Olympic team prior to the war. He swam all day, and somehow managed to make his way back to the wreckage of the *Tjisalak*.

But Blears wasn't the only one to have found the wreckage. Sharks in numbers had as well, and they were circling the water.

Then he heard someone shout to him. Across the circling sharks, it was from a life raft carrying four other survivors. Though Blears was by now utterly exhausted, he had never swum faster.

Blears made it into the raft and the five men tried to chart a course for Ceylon, more than 500 miles away. Their survival chances were still slim, but luck was finally with them. An American Liberty ship, the SS *James A. Wilder*, plucked them from the water. The British national, second wireless operator James Blears, was safe.

So I came to learn that my business partner, the man we'd come to know as Lord Tally Ho, the monocled, caped wrestler with the big handshake and the big heart, was one of the precious few from the *Tjisalak* who survived slaughter at the hands of the Japanese and a desperate swim in the shark-infested Indian Ocean.

Knowing Blears' story as I do now, it seems like the least I could've done to let him go surfing when he wanted to. ✦

In a June 1972 tag team match at the Civic, Gentleman Ed clamps a sleeper hold on King Crow as referee Wally Tsutsumi monitors the action.

CHAPTER 6

Stress Incorporated

As our wrestling business grew and our fan base expanded throughout the Islands, anyone who met me face to face might have noticed something: a nagging little sore that lingered right on the point of my chin.

No, I hadn't cut myself shaving. And it wasn't the stubborn remnant of all those years getting my face ground into the wrestling mat.

The sore seemed to mysteriously come and go on its own. After several doctors' consultations and a little soul-searching on my part, there was only one logical explanation: The appearance and disappearance of that little sore spot was directly related to the amount of stress I was feeling about the wrestling business.

The sore was present far more often than it wasn't.

I mentioned it to Lord Blears, and it should have been no surprise that he was similarly afflicted: The stress Blears was feeling manifested itself in the form of a persistent red spot on the right side of his neck.

Of course, we had little time to compare our respective stress points—we had next week's main event to plan!

For both of us, it was truly like King Sisyphus, the character in Greek mythology who was doomed to forever push a giant rock uphill, only to see it roll back down the hill and begin all over again. Every week's match was our rock to push up the hill, involving a collection of characters to mix, pair and position on the undercard, as well as the big rivalry between two (or more!) big stars to place and promote in the main-event slot.

The spot on my chin got a little bigger, and the spot on Blears' neck got a little redder, when we started planning and promoting the matches on the outer-islands along with our Oahu dates.

Part of the added challenge was delegating duties to folks we'd hired on the outer-islands to help set up the matches. They were all great people, but because Blears and I weren't on the outer islands for any length of time in advance of a match, we flew blind a little bit, and relied on our outer island surrogates to promote the matches there and fill the houses.

It was an interesting collection of "managers" we collected to help us make the outer island matches happen. On the Big Island, our Hilo and Kona promoters were both Chinese, and one of them was a dock supervisor by day. On Maui, our promoter was actually the head of the prison system there. On Kauai, we had an Army National Guard sergeant running the show. Each got a small percentage of the house, and we got the help we so desperately needed.

The added venues in Conroy Bowl at Schofield Barracks and Pearl Harbor's Bloch Arena meant more stress. We'd gotten into Conroy Bowl because a sergeant there was a huge wrestling fan and had an in with all the colonels and generals, so he did the lobbying on our behalf. To gain entry to the Bloch Arena venue, a referee of ours named Peter Peterson was a recovering alcoholic, and he had started AA for the staff at Pearl Harbor. He got us the green light there.

The key in my mind, as I kept pacing and rubbing that spot on my chin, was to always keep moving forward, growing, building the business in some way to avoid getting complacent and losing our momentum, then losing the fans.

We even started making "road trips" to put on matches for the folks on Guam. This got started because the owner of the first TV station we were on, Bob Berger, had a small station on Guam and knew the right people to get us started.

Even a little venue like Guam created new stress points for me. As we tried to hammer out the deal to put on matches there, I was informed that Guam had an athletic commission. The commission expected me to bring our wrestlers in a week early, with the ostensible purpose of giving their doctors the chance to examine them and sanction the matches.

But I sensed that the real reason for them to require our early arrival was simply to generate revenue for the island. Their commission running our operation meant more of our time on the island, staying in their hotels, eating their food, renting their cars. It translated to more money for Guam.

With tight schedules and small profit margins, there was no way I could accede to their demand to bring our wrestlers in a week early. If I wanted matches on Guam, I knew I had to find some way to work around the athletic commission.

So I hatched a plot. I invited all the key players on Guam to a big dinner, to discuss our plans together. I laid in a good stock of booze, expensive cigars and a huge spread of food. The commissioners arrived and drank and ate and drank some more. By the time they were all well-oiled and feeling no pain, I was able to make a deal with them to let us in without their week's grace period.

Sometimes a little well-placed liquid hospitality goes a long way.

But as the head of Mid-Pacific Promotions—a.k.a. "Stress Incorporated"—I honestly can't remember a day in the Islands that I wasn't worrying about our business.

I'd even panic if I was out in public, maybe for a meal with my family or a meeting with Lord Blears, and no one came up to me or recognized me. No, it wasn't that I was hungry for the attention. I just worried that if I was on TV every week in homes throughout the Islands, and no one was acknowledging me in public, then maybe they weren't watching.

I know. I'm a worrywart. But I couldn't help it.

All of our best plotting, all of our best promotion on a wrestling night could be undone by one simple slap from the cruel hand of Mother Nature. Lord Blears and I could devise the greatest lineup of action-packed matches our crowd could possibly hope for, only to discover that the house was barely half-full, because of the rain.

I could never figure out why it was. If it rained, the Hawaii fans would stay away. It always seemed so strange to me. After all, the rain in Hawaii is often nothing more than "liquid sunshine." The clouds would blow through from the mountaintops, and the Civic or our military-base venues or outer-island stops would get a light, fresh washing from above that was over as quickly as it started.

It was nothing like the icy rains I'd been through on the Mainland, like daggers through your clothes, or, worse, the driving snowstorms that blanketed and crippled neighborhoods, airports and entire cities. Truly bad weather I could understand. It would make me want to stay home, too.

But a little Hawaiian rain? There was nothing I could do about it, even though I tried.

For some strange reason, I had it in my head that the ancient Hawaiians stacked stones to win the favor of their gods. So, if the weather was threatening at all on the nights before a big match, I'd superstitiously start stacking stones in little piles outside my door, to honor the gods and ward off the rain.

It never worked. I guess all the Hawaiian gods—right along with my wife, Arlene—really didn't care for all those rocks piled up around the house. So I'd make my way through the rain, down to the wrestling venue, only to find once again that our decent box office that night had been rained out, literally.

I was constantly pacing back and forth at home at night or during the day at my office, just trying to dream up "high spots"—stunts or turns in the ring that would elicit a big crowd reaction. I came up with one in a match where

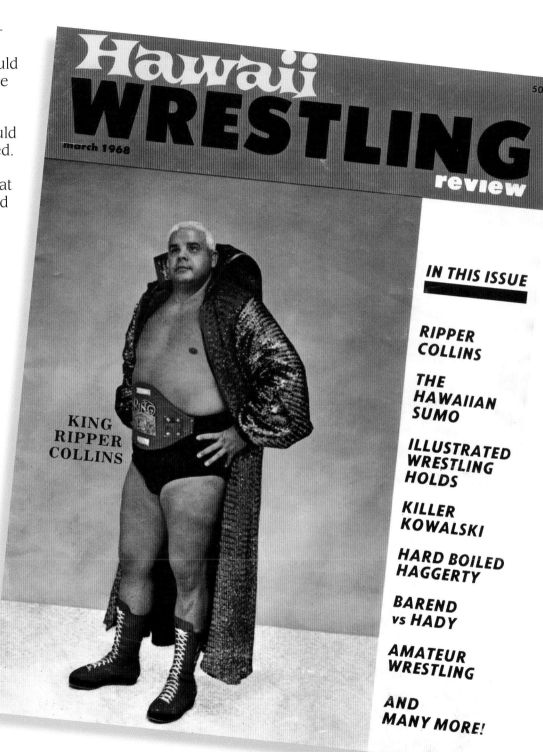

Hawaii WRESTLING review

march 1968

50¢

KING RIPPER COLLINS

IN THIS ISSUE

RIPPER COLLINS

THE HAWAIIAN SUMO

ILLUSTRATED WRESTLING HOLDS

KILLER KOWALSKI

HARD BOILED HAGGERTY

BAREND vs HADY

AMATEUR WRESTLING

AND MANY MORE!

41

against another duo that included the man Hawaii truly loved to hate, Ripper Collins.

Ripper had been working me over pretty good, and he had me down on the floor outside the ring. Then I got some help (probably despite the ref's protests) from my partner Sammy. He came up behind Ripper and held him, pinning his arms so Ripper was helpless.

This gave me the perfect opportunity to do what the fans had been hoping for all match—to haul off and deck Ripper. I wound up my biggest roundhouse and, as Sammy held Ripper up to take his punishment, I came in for the kill.

But at the last possible instant, as I swung with all my might at Ripper, he ducked. The audience roared when they saw the force of my blow land squarely on the side of Sammy's head, dropping him to the cement floor in a heap. Fans were screaming at Sammy to get up, screaming at me for what I'd done, screaming at Ripper the villain, who'd escaped certain harm and now strutted around the ring like a stuffed peacock.

The sound of the crowd that night, and the instant realization that we'd managed to give the fans their money's worth—that was the ultimate stress reliever for Gentleman Ed Francis.

But what do you do as a follow-up? Next week just kept coming, always too quickly.

In the "I-hit-Sammy-instead-of-Ripper" saga, Sam Steamboat and I got into a nasty argument in the locker room about whose fault it all was. Sammy, of course, blamed me for hitting him, and I blamed Sammy for not having the sense to get out of the way.

How do you settle an argument? For us, it was with one simple line in the locker room: "Why don't we settle this in the ring?" And, bingo, just like that— "Francis vs. Steamboat Grudge Match" becomes next week's main event.

Though Lord Blears and I worked hard to create these "water-cooler" moments with all our wrestlers in the ring—big moments that the fans might be talking about the next day at the office or with friends—I actually tried to limit the fans' direct interaction with the wrestlers. As strange as it sounds, I always tried to keep my wrestlers stashed in the locker room rather than letting them go out with the fans.

Of course, we had numerous sanctioned "meet-and-greet" events at which the fans could see the wrestlers live and in person. I staged several of them at Ala Moana Center, in a little courtyard area under the staircase where fans could gather around to watch demonstrations, get autographs and shake hands with our guys.

But those appearances I could (to some degree) control. It was different if the wrestlers wanted to go out in the stands during our wrestling cards, to see the other matches or sit with fans. I tried to discourage that.

Why?

It's kind of like the "Great Almighty Wizard of Oz" in the classic movie. Behind the curtain, the Wizard was just a man, a mere mortal. In my mind, it was the same with our wrestlers. Up in the ring and on our televised interviews, they were larger-than-life personas.

Those characters were the foundation, the

building blocks of our escapist entertainment. I felt that it was important for the fans to see them as those characters in order for the audience to get swept along by our fairy tale every week.

Without the mystery, the Wizard of Oz lost his powers. I didn't want that to happen with my wrestlers. No peeking behind the curtain.

With all the day-to-day demands of our wrestling business, the notion of a true vacation always seemed out of the question for me. My wife, Arlene, would suggest it from time to time, but I'd always say, "Where would you want to go on vacation? We live in Hawaii. This is a vacation!"

The one bit of time off I actually took during the Hawaii wrestling years was when I made plans to buy a car in Oregon. It was a gorgeous Cadillac convertible, the car of my dreams, and its powerful allure made me willing to leave my desk in Honolulu for a few days. I agreed to take Arlene, with the idea that we'd turn the car-buying expedition into a nice little Mainland getaway. The plan was to buy the car, use it to tour and enjoy Oregon, then travel home and have the car shipped back to us.

At the airport in Honolulu before our flight to Oregon, I began feeling very ill. I might have come down with some sort of bug. But I suspect the real "bug" was just the prospect of being away from the business for any time at all. I'd never done it before. My stomach was turning inside out.

Arlene talked me onto the plane, and we got the car in Oregon and spent a bit of time there. But for the trip home, we'd booked passage on the Matson liner out of San Francisco. Once we boarded the ship and headed out from port, I felt like a caged animal. It seemed to me that it was taking forever to cross the Pacific. I kept thinking to myself, "Is this as fast as this thing can go?"

*Ed and Sam Steamboat (right) built on the "Ed-hits-Sam-instead-of-Ripper" incident with a grudge match the following week.
Opposite: Ed absorbs a blow from Ripper Collins.*

We finally made it back to Honolulu. My desk, my wrestlers, the TV studio never looked so good. That was the only time off I ever took. I guess I just wasn't really the vacationing type. ◆

Velasco, the "phantom of the Civic," could fix it or clean it on demand—for wrestling matches or any other attraction. Here, the auditorium floor is reconfigured for a roller derby match in 1954. Opposite: Local companies like Holiday Mart supported events with wrestling-themed ads in programs and fan pubs.

CHAPTER 7

The Man in the Rafters

Even on the days that Lord Blears was out riding waves and I was on my own in our office, the Civic Auditorium was a wonderful place to come to work.

Sure, it was old. It was in need of repairs in every musty corner. But Honolulu's Civic was the kind of building that had history dripping from its walls. Over the previous 30-odd years before my tenure there, the palace on South King had housed great boxers, great wrestlers, great sumo masters, wild roller-derby stars, and many of the world's most famous singers and musical performers.

The Civic had a kind of lived-in smell that was a heady amalgam of its many years of use. It was a familiar but nonspecific aroma, a blend of cigars and cigarettes, sweat and soy sauce, dirt and grime and human traffic.

The building's bulging, cavernous shape, illuminated by big scoop lights hung up in the grid high above, was reminiscent of the best of all the wrestling venues I'd passed through around the country.

When you walked off King Street and into the Civic, there was a distinct aura that surrounded you and spoke to you. It said:

Come in.

Take a seat.

You're with friends.

We're all going to see a show
Like none we've ever seen before.

The Civic was the right size. It was big enough to stage an event, a show or a concert or a match that carried some import and excitement with it. But it wasn't so big as to make each fan feel detached, diminished. There was an enduring intimacy that made every fan's experience special and memorable.

The man who owned the Civic, Louis Rosen, became a close and lifelong friend of mine. Lou was an interesting mixture of generosity and cautiousness with his money, maybe because, like me, he

45

came from Chicago in the tough times, when money was scarce but we helped each other.

On the one hand, as to his generosity, Lou once flew his Beverly Hills tailor in to Hawaii, just to make a suit for my young son Sonny. On the other hand, when Lou and his wife came to the Islands and stayed at the penthouse of the Moana Hotel, if they needed to do some laundry, his wife would call my wife and come do it out at our house, to avoid the hotel cleaning fee.

For one star-studded gala event in Honolulu that the Rosens attended, Lou's wife went to Liberty House and bought a beautiful new dress to wear. They went to the party that night and Lou's wife looked fabulous. Then the next day she took the dress back to Liberty House, said she didn't like it and got her money back. I guess habits born in the Depression die hard.

The Civic had a kind of homespun folksiness that was endearing. But I discovered that even it required a watchful eye.

Fans that came to our matches at the Civic first bought their tickets, and then were asked to slip the stubs into the slot on top of a collection box at the door. After our matches I'd compare our "take," the cash we were bringing in, with the official box-office tally at the door.

Something wasn't adding up. It took me a little while, and a spy on the premises, to discover that a good number of our wrestling fans were, in fact, con artists.

It turned out that some resourceful souls were actually tearing off pieces of matchbooks, covering them with their thumbs and sliding their own homemade "tickets" into the slot. They hadn't bought tickets at all. I was putting freebies in the seats.

I began to wonder: Was there anything, any part of this operation that I didn't have to worry about?

One thing that went off without a hitch at the old Civic was its upkeep and maintenance. That's because the Civic had Velasco.

It was in the first few days after I'd opened my office inside the Civic that I learned about Velasco. Initially, I didn't meet him or see him so much as hear him, somewhere in the distance, high up in the rafters of the Civic, tinkering, working, fixing.

He was a shadowy figure I knew only from afar at first, a phantom: the true Phantom of the Civic. For Velasco quite literally lived in the Civic Auditorium.

And he was just Velasco. He wasn't Buddy Velasco, or Clyde Velasco, or Vincent Velasco. I only ever heard Ralph Yempuku and the other fixtures around the Civic refer to Velasco by the one single name.

Yempuku allowed Velasco to live at the Civic, in return for Velasco's full-time services as the facility's janitor and handyman. One day in my knocking around the doors and passages of the Civic I discovered that Velasco actually had a bed in the back, in a small sort of storage room.

(Suffice it to say that the little room would have made an excellent laboratory testing ground for a company like Febreze to test its odor-masking products.)

In time I did get to meet Velasco face to face. He was an industrious little Portuguese guy of indeterminate age—maybe early 40s?—who said very little but was truly devoted to the care and cleaning of the arena. There was an endless succession of burned-out auditorium lights to change. There were loose ceiling tiles to tack down. There were aisles to sweep, trash to haul away, broken folding chairs to fix.

Whenever Yempuku or myself would stumble across anything that needed attending to in the storied old Civic, the call would echo through the facility: "Velaaaasco!!"

No phone, no text, no email. Just a shout, and Velasco was on it.

No matter what hour of the day or night I was in the facility, planning matches or staging them, checking the venue or checking the crowd, starting my workday or ending it, I'd see him. There was Velasco, toiling in the dark with a work lamp, sweeping, cleaning, hauling.

Velasco had one great brush with celebrity. In June 1963, U.S. President John F. Kennedy made a stop in Hawaii, and his motorcade drove through Honolulu. To commemorate the grand event, Velasco went out and put up the president's name in big, bold letters on the Civic Auditorium marquee facing King Street.

Only one small problem: Velasco didn't take down the letters that were already up there, promoting our upcoming wrestling match.

So passersby at 1314 South King Street saw John F. Kennedy vs. and then the rest of our wrestlers' names for the card we were promoting.

It made it look like we had a brand-new wrestler in our stable for the upcoming card: a guy named John F. Kennedy. The local papers had a field day with it, sending a photographer down to document the president's top billing on our wrestling card, and Velasco's handiwork was immortalized in print the next day.

I only recall Velasco complaining to me once. He knew I was the top dog for the wrestling matches, and the matches were the bane of Velasco's existence. That's because after our fans were done jumping around and shouting at our matches, but before they left the Civic, they dropped things. Lots of things. They dropped soda cups. They dropped hot dog wrappers. They dropped cigars and cigarette butts.

And it all ended up on the floor. Velasco's floor.

So one Thursday morning, as Velasco was once again sweeping up the piles of trash after a Wednesday-night match, I happened to walk by him.

I could feel Velasco's eyes on me. He'd stopped sweeping and was just leaning on his broom, looking at me.

"What?" I said.

Velasco gestured to the mountain of trash at his feet.

"Dis," he said. "Too much. Every week, too much."

I understood his discontent. I wouldn't want to be sweeping up all that stuff every week either.

"Yeah, it's bad," I said. "But what do you want me to do?"

Velasco thought about it for a moment. Then he pointed to the P.A. system hanging in the Civic.

"Make an announcement," Velasco suggested. "'No t'row stuff on da floor!'"

I promised Velasco we'd try to make it better. But no announcement was going to slow down our fans.

So Velasco's chores continued, stretching across decades in the Civic. I had moved into my office there in 1961, when Velasco and I first met. And though the brand-new Honolulu International Center—later called the Neal S. Blaisdell Center—opened just three years later, in 1964, the old Civic continued to play host to our wrestling and other events until it finally closed its doors and was torn down in 1974.

As far as I knew, Velasco had lived in the Civic long before I arrived, and continued living there till the very end. It was odd: In the entire time Velasco was working the floors or climbing through the rafters of the Civic, I never saw him set foot in the arena's front offices.

I don't know what happened to Velasco when the grand old Civic was torn down, his bed and bedroom no doubt unceremoniously turned into rubble by a bulldozer. Now, so many years later, I've long since lost touch with him. It's likely that Velasco has passed on from our world.

If so, I know one thing for certain. If God needs a light bulb changed up there, Velasco is on it. ◆

Five thousand fans pack the Civic in May 1967 to watch an evening of wrestling inside a barbed-wire-topped enclosure, including a tag team match pitting Ripper Collins and Curtis Iaukea against Jim Hady and Handsome Johnny Barend—an event billed as "Four Men Locked in a Steel Cage." Opposite: In 1964 the Honolulu International Center opened on the site of the old Ward Estate.

Chapter 8

The Last Man Standing

It was a steady building process.

With our shows at the Civic, on the outer islands and at the military bases, our Mid-Pacific Promotions was attracting big-name wrestlers who could deliver crowd-pleasing main events for our fans.

Then, in 1964, we had one huge, ripe mango hanging in front of us, just waiting to be picked: A beautiful new facility was about to open its doors for the people of Hawaii.

It was a promoter's dream come true. The new Honolulu International Center (HIC), on the old Ward estate property, bordered by Ward Avenue on the Ewa side and King and Kapiolani streets on the mauka and makai sides, could seat almost 9,000 people for sports events like ours, compared to the under 6,000 that fit in the Civic.

The entire new complex was a jewel in the crown of Honolulu's sports and spectator-entertainment scene. The main arena, along with the adjacent concert hall, would house basketball and ice skating, concerts and trade shows, symphonies and commencement ceremonies. It was to become the true centerpiece of Oahu event life.

Guess what? No surprise. I wanted my wrestlers in there.

And, of course, I'd be able to make that happen, right? After all, with a good solid three years of promoting history under my belt in the

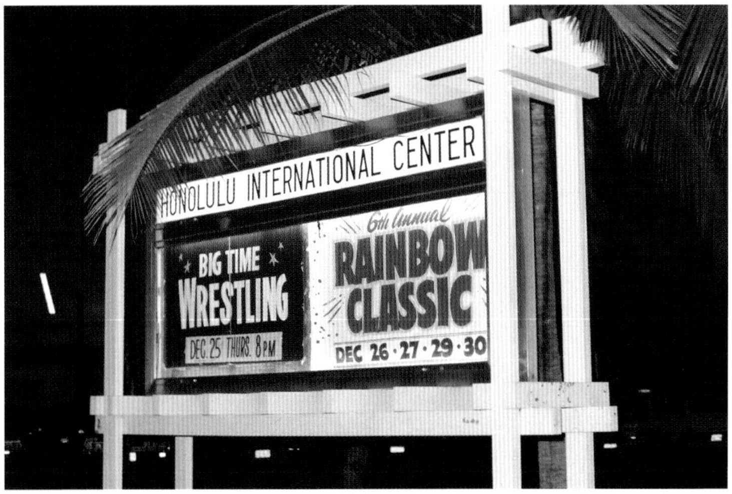

Islands, since 1961, bringing in top-drawing cards every week, complemented by our hourlong weekly show on Channel 4, who'd say no to me?

The City of Honolulu, that's who.

Even though it was an unwritten law in wrestling circles that promoters paid for and were given territorial rights in their respective regions—Los Angeles, New York, Chicago, Texas, Hawaii and so on—the City of Honolulu didn't see it that way. Because the new HIC facility was owned and operated by the City, its decision was not to honor my promotional rights in the Islands, and instead to put the rights to book wrestling matches into their venue up for bid.

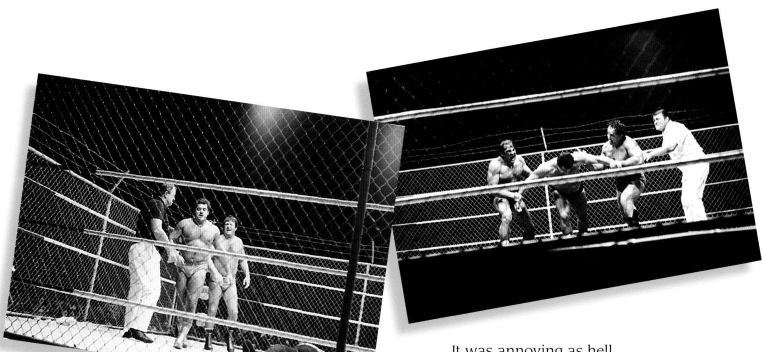

You can't fight City Hall, right?

So the process went out to bid, and I lost to a car salesman.

A man named Dallas Western was a successful car dealer who had his eye on pro wrestling. Even though he didn't really know wrestling or wrestlers, I guess he figured he knew a good business opportunity when he saw it.

So Western contacted a former wrestler named Roy Shire to help him with his new "dream venture" in Hawaii. I didn't know Western, but Shire was a man I knew well.

Maybe a little too well. As in "bad-blood" well.

Shire and I had some history years earlier when we were both wrestling in Ohio. At the time, he wrestled under the moniker "Professor Roy Shire," and he had a cane that he carried around with him. He'd go into promoters' offices with that cane, making demands on them, tapping their desks with his cane to get his way.

It was annoying as hell.

To make matters worse, with all his cockiness and arrogance, he actually thought he was a great wrestler. He wasn't. I knew who the other true shooters were. We were the guys who trained seriously first as amateur wrestlers, who weren't just play-acting, who could put a hurt on you that would stick. "Professor" Roy Shire wasn't one of us.

But in the ring one night in Ohio, Shire thought he could show me a few things. He began acting up in his cocky way, jerking me around, messing with the direction of our match. This went on until I got fed up. I took Shire, flipped him over my head, took him down, slammed down on top of him and then said quietly in his ear, so the fans couldn't hear, "Okay, Professor. You want to work, or you want to shoot?"

I'd called his bluff. He behaved. But he didn't see the need to like me much after that. The feeling was entirely mutual.

So this man—one of the few I'd ever had bad blood with in my career—was partnered with Dallas Western to try to move into the Hawaii territory for wrestling promotion at the Honolulu

International Center. Shire had a wrestling TV show in the San Francisco Bay area, featuring some good names like Ray Stevens, Edward Carpenter, Kenji Shibuya, Pepper Gomez and others. They knew exactly what I'd been doing successfully in the Islands for the past three years, both at the Civic and on TV.

I'm sure they figured the wrestling goose in Hawaii could lay some more golden eggs. Why not for them?

It was a blind, sealed bid for the wrestling rights at the HIC, and after Blears and I discussed it and I lost some more sleep, I submitted a bid that seemed more than fair.

It wasn't enough.

Western and Shire outbid me and, though it didn't seem possible, this amazing new facility in Honolulu would open its doors for wrestlers other than mine, wrestling for Dallas Western and his new company, Aloha Promotions. They were awarded the rights by the City of Honolulu.

It was like a bad dream.

And from the start, it led to a serious turf war.

The first salvo in the war came on July 28, 1964. Two things happened in Honolulu that night. First, it was the night of Dallas Western's premiere wrestling show at the HIC. With Roy Shire's help, they'd, of course, pulled out all the stops, staging five prelim matches then his "main event," a U.S. Heavyweight Championship match between champ Ray Stevens and challenger Ed Carpenter.

But on the very same night, there was another wrestling match for Hawaii fans to attend, just about a half mile Diamond Head on King Street at Civic Auditorium. That match featured an amazing, unbelievable, incredible 18-Man Texas Battle Royal featuring Curtis Iaukea, Luther Lindsay, Tosh Togo, Gene Kiniski, Mr. Moto and many other enormously talented wrestlers.

What a coincidence. Who do you suppose promoted that fantastic night of wrestling at the old Civic, on the same night as the HIC debut?

Hey, what did you expect? This was war.

I guess that first battle in the war had to be called a draw. Both wrestling shows sold out that

night, at the HIC and the Civic. In total, more than 14,000 fans paid to see wrestling on that single night in Honolulu.

The war raged on this way for a series of dates, with me scheduling matches at every opportunity to go head to head with theirs, to try to draw away any fan base they might hope to build. Call it our very own Hawaii Promoters Death Match, with the spoils going to the last man standing.

On those nights of dueling matches, I'd put up giant searchlights out on King Street in front of the Civic, beaming their lights up into the sky over Honolulu. I figured, that way, any wrestling fan driving by who hadn't yet bought a ticket might be lured to our product.

It should have been no surprise that our turf war, like all wars, turned into a mean, ugly business.

Among the many friends I now had in Hawaii in the early '60s, one close friend of mine happened to work at the airlines. So one week I did a little research, and I found out which plane flight several of Western and Shire's wrestlers were taking from the Mainland to Hawaii.

All it took was one well-placed phone call. When the wrestlers arrived, they went strolling over to baggage claim in Honolulu Airport, but, mysteriously, the airline had lost their bags. All of them.

Their match was that night. Their wrestling clothes were in their luggage.

Do you have any idea how tough it is to find a red-sequined men's speedo, size extra-extra-large, on short notice in Honolulu? Or size 16 wrestling boots? Very difficult, trust me. I checked.

Television became the next battleground in the war. Western and Shire managed to get a slot on KONA-TV, Channel 2, in Honolulu, airing shows weekly to promote their matches. Our show on Channel 4 continued airing on Sunday afternoons. Even I had to concede, it was a lot of wrestling for Hawaii. Something had to give.

Something did, in 1965.

A lawsuit was filed against Dallas Western, by the talent agency he used to fly wrestlers in to Hawaii for his matches. When Lord Blears and I learned of it, we had to smile. We were our own talent agency. The guys we brought in were all friends, or friends of friends. We made the calls. We sent the letters. No talent agency. No talent-agency fees.

But I guess Western—the car dealer—had needed to use an outside agency to bring the talent in, promising to pay them for services rendered. From the claims in the suit, it appeared he hadn't exactly held up his end of the bargain.

I don't mean to gloat. Ah, what the hell. I will.

The lesson to be learned is: When what you know is cars, you don't try to traffic in wrestlers.

As for Shire? He was still looming on the edges of our operation in the Islands. And unlike Western the car guy, Shire wasn't a complete out-sider. He'd been a wrestler. He knew wrestlers.

In fact, right around that time I saw Shire at one of the big National Wrestling Alliance meetings in Las Vegas. I certainly wasn't looking to make him my best buddy in the world, but I remembered the old saying: Keep your friends close, and your enemies closer.

So, in the elevator in a Vegas hotel, I extend-ed the olive branch to Shire. I held out my hand to him and said, "Listen. Let's work together instead of bumping heads. Why don't you share your wrestlers with me, and we'll make it work as a team, without Dallas Western?"

Shire agreed, and we went forward. I man-aged to put the bad blood between Shire and myself behind us for the sake of the business in Hawaii and my family. As always, the success of the business came first.

Western's promotion operation in Hawaii folded fairly quickly after that. In March 1965, Mid-Pacific Promotions and our 50th State Wrestling staged their first wrestling card at the Honolulu International Center. The main event featured Curtis

Iaukea going
up against Giant Baba.

I don't recall who won.

I just recall that it was glorious.

The HIC felt enormous. While the Civic was lived-in and worn, the HIC was bright, new, clean. While the Civic was middle-aged, feeling the creak in its bones, the HIC was a baby, less than a year old and still with that new-car smell.

The only thing I missed was Velasco.

I will confess that the monthly matches we began presenting in our new, more spacious digs at the HIC were a constant source of panic for me. Can we draw a big enough crowd? Will the people come?

In Billy Francis' first professional fight, at the HIC Arena on Christmas 1969, he and Ed team up against Ripper Collins and his "valet," Friday Allman. Here, Collins restrains Billy while Allman has a hammer lock on Ed. Opposite: On the same card, Hahn Lee uses the ropes against Danny Hodge as referee Pete Peterson looks on.

If you had come to any of those HIC matches and you were looking for me, you'd probably find me leaning up against a palm tree on the Pensacola Street side of the parking lot. I'd take a position there and watch for the cars coming in. I'd look at my watch, look at the parking lot entrance booth and, as the minutes ticked by toward showtime, I'd sweat more and more.

A packed parking lot on sellout nights was very gratifying. Those were the dates when, if the advance ticket sales were strong enough, I got to call the newspapers and have them change our ad to read "Sold Out." But what about next week?

I had very little time to revel in the glory of our new digs. My next sumo-sized worry was already looming, rain clouds on the horizon.

Our TV show on Channel 4 had helped our business tremendously. I saw the gate explode at the Civic, and I knew it would be the same at the HIC.

Or, I thought I knew.

In short order I got word that Bob Berger, the station owner at KHVH-TV, had decided not to extend a yearlong contract with us. Whether it was economics, other station priorities or the inconvenience of having our rickety, makeshift ring cluttering up his studio, the decision was made to not continue our show.

I saw my dream and our meal ticket once again fading away, threatening to take me back to where I'd been when I arrived in the Islands, with no TV deal.

But at this juncture there was one significant difference. While before I had had nothing, now I had history. I was a proven commodity. I had a track record of TV success and an eager crowd at the Civic and the HIC. I was in a much stronger bargaining position than I had been before. I was a better "package."

Just when I needed it again, more good fortune.

Over at KGMB-TV, Channel 9, a man named Cec Heftel was now running the ship. With his Heftel Broadcasting acquiring KGMB, he was hell-bent on making it the preeminent TV power in the Islands. He packaged the TV station with KGMB-AM and KGMB-FM radio to make a mini-broadcasting empire for the Island audience.

Best of all, from where I sat? Heftel liked wrestling.

I can't say whether Heftel was himself a wrestling fan, but he recognized its merit for his audience: the excitement, the action, the fan devotion. I brought with me an attorney recommended by my old friends Lou and Herman Rosen—the father-son team that owned the Civic and the Royal Theaters chain—for a meeting in Heftel's office, to help me pitch the move for our wrestling show to KGMB.

It turned out that Cec had big plans for wrestling. He was building a powerhouse news operation at the station, bringing in newsman Bob Sevey to anchor it, and he wanted to position our wrestling show in adjacency to the news to drive viewers in the right direction.

We made a deal. Our TV show was on its way to KGMB, to be called 50th State Big-Time Wrestling. We'd ultimately get slots on Friday nights

after the news, and on Saturday afternoons before the news.

This, in itself, was a very big deal, because in the TV business a station rises or falls on the success of its news operation. For Heftel to place us on his schedule adjacent to the news, either to drive viewer traffic to the newscasts, or to receive the station's viewership following them, was a big vote of confidence in our product.

To sweeten the deal—thanks in no small part to the negotiating skill of the Rosens' attorney friend—Heftel agreed to give me a percentage of the revenues from the commercials sold in our shows.

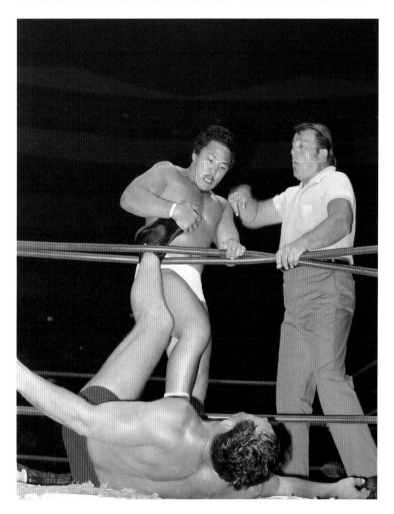

That part of the arrangement was new to me, and I wasn't complaining.

Once we'd sealed the deal and I walked out of Heftel's office, I couldn't feel the pavement on Kapiolani Boulevard under my feet. Was this really happening?

Indeed it was.

Of course, with the new TV deal in place and our state-of-the-art, tricked-out home at the HIC, the heat was on me more than ever to produce great, big events: huge promotions to serve up great crowd-pleasing matches with bad blood, grudges and high stakes smeared all over the wrestling card.

In an effort to make some of these matches a true celebration for Hawaii fans, I took a gamble and started scheduling them on other big celebratory days like Christmas Day and Thanksgiving Day. Everyone told me I was crazy. It had never been done before, anywhere in the nation. They all said fans would be busy with their holidays, and would shy away from our matches on those days.

But I reasoned: What do you do after you open your presents or have your dinner on Christmas? Or after you have your Thanksgiving dinner early in the day? Odds are, the family is together and you're not working. Why not go watch wrestling?

Am I right? I must be right. Right?

If you attended any of those holiday matches at the HIC, early in the day you would have seen one anxious promoter with a furrowed brow, nervously pacing around the HIC parking lot, counting cars as they came in. For those events I'd lie awake at night: What if no one shows up?

But I was delighted and rewarded to see the fans show up in droves. Those matches on Christmas and Thanksgiving were some of our very largest houses, complete sellouts, and the Christmas Day 50th State Big-Time Wrestling Match at the HIC became a holiday tradition for many Hawaii families. Many promoters across the Mainland got wind of our success, and began following our lead and scheduling their own holiday matches.

In the face of everyone's advice to stay away from those special holidays, I felt thoroughly vindicated in my gamble. I got a little swagger in my step, and got just a bit too full of myself over my great all-knowing skill as a promoter. One year, I decided to schedule a big main-event match at the HIC on Mother's Day.

After all, I figured, every other holiday was proving to be a big success. Families would be together on Mother's Day—what better outing than to pack everyone up and take Mom to the wrestling matches?

So there I was, pacing the parking lot in the HIC on Mother's Day, saying to myself (or maybe even muttering aloud), They'll come. I know they'll come. They'll be here any minute now.

But they didn't come.

The Mother's Day HIC wrestling promotion was a huge bomb. About my unparalleled skill as a promoter, I was brought quickly back down to Earth. I learned the hard way that maybe moms weren't exactly the heart and soul of our wrestling audience. I didn't do that again.

Live and learn!

Somehow, by the same kind of trial and error, I figured out what worked and what didn't work for the Hawaii fans. For the most part, even trying to fill the bigger HIC venue, it was working. There were many, many weeks where I'd taken out an ad in the *Star-Bulletin* or the *Advertiser* for the week's matches, only to have to call the papers and tell them to change the ad to "Sold Out." It was a wonderful problem to have.

The other thing I learned, through constant plotting with Lord Blears, was how to juggle our match cards to get the maximum fan response to them.

Danny Hodge shows off his junior world heavyweight championship belt at the HIC Arena on Christmas 1969. Hodge retained the title after wrestling Hahn Lee to a draw. Opposite: The Sheik and Gene Kiniski are escorted to the ring before their October 1971 tag team victory over Peter Maivia and Curtis Iaukea.

57

The questions were always: Who do I put on in the first match, the second match? Who do I bring up through the ranks to become a big star? Who do I put in the semifinal so that maybe he could wrestle the champ next week? I'd have to be orchestrating this in my mind as I put together the card every week.

Generally speaking, it was the "showmen" who accelerated up the card toward the big money faster than the "shooters." Big, bawdy showmen like Ripper or The Missing Link got the biggest fan reaction. But that didn't mean I could put them up to wrestle, week after week. Why would you go back next week and see the same guys do the same thing?

It's like having a tuna sandwich. I like tuna. I like tuna sandwiches. But if I had to eat a tuna sandwich every day, every meal, without a break? I know I'd hate tuna.

So it was that I had to constantly be changing it up, bringing new faces, new drama, new hostilities between the wrestlers to keep the fan interest going.

Very often my solution for any of the wrestlers was: go away. I realized in short order that I couldn't keep putting main-event guys like Curtis Iaukea, Neff Maiava or Ripper Collins at the end of the evening every week. Even with many of the prelim guys—I couldn't build an undercard with the same names over and over.

But it was difficult. I felt a responsibility to my wrestlers. I wasn't about to say to them, "Gee, we really can't use you this week, so go sit on the beach without drawing a paycheck."

That's why Lord Blears and I would reach out to our promoter friends on the Mainland, in Japan, in Australia, anywhere we could think of, to offer our wrestlers for some unspecified period of time.

This proved to be a "win-win" for all parties involved. My guys were getting paid in other regions. My fans were getting a break from the same diet, to increase their appetite for our stars' eventual return. The promoters we'd deal our guys to would reciprocate, sending us new faces, new blood, new stories to excite the Hawaii fans.

It was almost like we knew what we were doing. Even though we were making it up as we went.

Running matches out of the old Civic, the big new HIC and all our ancillary venues simultaneously required constant vigilance. Sometimes things would fall through the cracks.

One of those "cracks," I came to find, was some ticket skimming that had been going on under my nose at the HIC. A gentleman who had previously promoted roller derby at the Civic Auditorium became the head of the ticket office at the HIC, and was in charge of the box office for the big, new venue.

I only knew that we were putting butts in the seats, and we were making money. I thought all was good. But, much later, a "spy"—actually, a woman who worked in ticketing at the Civic and knew the fellow from his roller-derby days there—told me what had really gone on over at the HIC.

Much to my surprise, I learned that the head of ticketing at the HIC had been taking 100 or so tickets for our wrestling matches every week. They were front-row seats, the best and highest priced in the house. Then he'd sell them on the side and pocket the money.

I only found out about it after he'd already left the position at the HIC. My spy had refrained from telling me while he was there, fearful of what I might do.

Looking back, she probably made a good choice. It would not have been pretty. It would have likely involved some of my time in the mayor's office getting help putting a stop to the skimming, and perhaps a criminal prosecution.

Nobody told me it would be this complicated. ♦

KGMB-TV positioned 50th State Big-Time Wrestling right after the evening news with Bob Sevey on Friday nights. Opposite: Harry Fujiwara started his wrestling career in Hawaii in 1962 and changed his professional name to Mr. Fuji after moving to the East Coast to wrestle in the '70s.

FRIDAY
ED FRANCIS PRESENTS
9

FIRST TIME ON TV!
HAWAIIAN CHAMPIONSHIP WRESTLING MATCH

KING RIPPER COLLINS
Holder of Ring Magazine's Gold Belt

BATTLES

EDDIE MORRO
French star from Martinique

Plus
TAG TEAM WRESTLING
Handsome Johnny Barend and Hans Mortier
vs.
Jim Hady and Mr. America

TONIGHT 10:45 P.M. 9kgmb
Following the news

590 9kgmb

Chief Billy White Wolf, accompanied by Little Beaver at left, signs autographs for fans in June 1968.

CHAPTER 9

Rogues Gallery

Though I continued to stew and fret week after week, and to pace circles around Lord Blears, our Mid-Pacific Promotions wrestling mini-empire had somehow managed to become a respected fixture for Hawaii fans, as well as a modest success.

My biggest contribution was probably my sheer, bull-headed force of will. I was devoted to the business slavishly, night and day, because the alternative—allowing it to fail—was simply not an option.

Lord Blears' contribution came from his upbeat outlook and his wealth of wrestling contacts, worth their weight in gold. His years in wrestling made him irreplaceable as a booker of talent, and his winning way opened doors and cemented deals.

And of course, the true success of the operation depended on one simple ingredient that was always like picking low-hanging fruit for us: booking great wrestling talent to come to Hawaii.

With the combined pool of the guys Blears knew and the guys I knew, we had the available talent in the world of wrestling pretty well covered.

In the early going, most of the guys had never been to the Islands before. So to a man, whenever we'd call, I could hear on the other end of the phone that they felt exactly the way I did when Al Karasick first called me to wrestle in Hawaii: Really? Are you serious? And you'll send me a plane ticket? Let me think about it for, like, two seconds. Yeah, I'll be there!

Just as I did, they envisioned the beaches, the tropical paradise, the chance for a working vacation. They weren't about to say no.

And remember: The vast majority of the guys who had found their way to the wrestling profession in the first place had backgrounds and beginnings that were not so terribly different from mine.

For the most part, like me, these were not men from families of means who had things handed to them. These were hardscrabble guys who'd been in their fair share of fights as kids. They were tough guys from working-class, blue-collar neighborhoods who found their way to the gym as a sanctuary. They weren't pretty boys. They'd come by their big burly bodies and their physical strength as a means of survival rather than for the mirror.

The wrestling ring offered them an honest living. Sure, the weeks on the road were a grind, the travel was exhausting and the night-after-night toll on their bodies was extreme. But the sport paid the rent. It put food and beer on the table. It may not have been glamorous, but as journeyman working wrestlers, they got by.

For guys like this, Hawaii was a picture postcard in a novelty shop. It was a location for fanciful Hollywood movies. It was someone else's dream. It wasn't a place they could even imagine visiting—until Blears and I rang them up.

So it was no surprise that they said yes. And it was no surprise that what followed in most cases was an instant, love-at-first-sight connection between our wrestlers and the Islands. Most never wanted to leave.

As a result, from our beginnings in 1961 well into the late 1970s, Lord Blears and I collected an amazing roster of wild characters from across the continental U.S., Asia and even Europe to do battle weekly for the benefit of Island fans. The entire cast would number in the hundreds, but some of the most prominent names in our Rogues Gallery stand out in my mind.

And every great wrestler, of course, comes with a story...

CURTIS "THE BULL" IAUKEA

Curtis Iaukea was a great friend of mine— and he was the most charismatic man I've ever met in my life. People were simply drawn to him, taken in by his spell. With that unique charm of his, he always seemed to manage to get his way.

I'm the first to admit that he worked his particular brand of magic on me all the time. One day, he was casually telling me about how he was feeling tired, complaining just a bit about how he needed to get away. Of course, I didn't want my big star to be unhappy, so I agreed that perhaps a little time off would do him some good.

Then, with that same kind of casual, offhand manner, he began telling me about a cruise he'd heard about on a merchant ship. He spoke wistfully about it, about how much he'd enjoy getting the chance to get out of the Islands and see more of the world, to sort of recharge his batteries.

Slowly, surely, he brought me along with his idea that this cruise would be a great, therapeutic thing for him. Before I knew it, I heard myself telling Curtis that I'd pay for the damn thing. It wasn't in

the budget, it wasn't anything I owed him—but that was Curtis. He just had a way of working things out to his advantage.

So off he went on his cruise around the world on a merchant ship that only had about a dozen passengers on it. And I bankrolled Mr. Iaukea's Excellent Adventure—to the tune of around $3,000, a truly princely sum for a struggling local wrestling promoter.

Many years later, when my son Russ was running for Congress in the Islands, I saw Curtis and he reminded me about the trip. "Eh, Ed, that was a wonderful cruise you gave me!" Curtis said with a smile. "Yeah, it cost me a lot of dough!" I remembered.

(Maybe I was just a softie. I also spent about $4,000 to send Lord Blears and his wife to England. What was I thinking?)

I kept Curtis on or around the main event on countless wrestling cards, because I always knew I could count on him to deliver. Everything was almost effortless with Curtis. After coming out of Punahou School, the University of California at Berkeley and the pro football ranks, Curtis was quite used to succeeding at whatever he did.

His time in the wrestling ring was no exception. He consistently found his way to entertain, to engineer "high spots" in his matches and to completely engage his fans. Their love for Curtis "Da Bull" bordered on absolute worship. Like an A-Rod in baseball, a Peyton in football or a Lebron in basketball, Curtis Iaukea in the world of pro wrestling in Hawaii was truly a "franchise player."

As "The Bull," of course, Curtis was supposed to be the bull of the Islands, the top dog, the toughest guy in the land. We helped fuel that reputation every week. So the fans who loved Curtis absolutely worshipped him. But there were those "other" fans, the ones who wanted to see Curtis knocked off his pedestal.

The clearest evidence of this was the riot at the Civic in August 1961, when Curtis went up against Neff Maiava. The chaos at the arena, the violence, the arrests were all testimony to the blind, over-the-top devotion of these guys' fans.

Admittedly, much of it was cultural. The Hawaiians loved Curtis. The Samoans loved Neff. The Samoans weren't so keen about Curtis.

So it was that, one day, as I was sitting in my office at the Civic trying to dream up something for the next week's card, I witnessed a little "encounter of the Samoan kind" out on King Street.

Curtis had just left the auditorium to head home. But as I watched through the window from my vantage point in my office, I saw a couple of Samoan guys pull up in front of Curtis on motorcycles.

At first I thought they were all friends. It didn't take long for me to see I was wrong.

The Samoan guys stepped off their bikes, and Curtis spoke to them, gesturing as he spoke. I noticed that no one was smiling. Then one of the Samoan guys stepped up close to Curtis, violating his personal space. I could see the Samoan had some things on

In 1963 Iaukea played a character named Itchi Kitchi in the movie "The Three Stooges Go Around the World in a Daze."

ROGUES GALLERY

his mind that he wanted to share with Curtis. Those things definitely weren't about how good-looking he thought Curtis was.

Curtis held a hand up to the Samoan who'd stepped close to him, and took a small step back. I couldn't hear what they were saying, but it looked to me as though Curtis was kind of begging off a fight. They had a few more words.

Curtis told me later what they were saying to him, and what he said in return.

"Oh, you t'ink you da Bull?" the Samoans said to him. "You not so tough ..."

"Eh, brah, I don' want any trouble," Curtis said. "Not on 'dis nice day ... You two guys out on your beautiful motorcycles ..."

(Curtis spoke pidgin only when and where it was appropriate. He didn't get into Punahou and Cal Berkeley speaking pidgin.)

Next, Curtis looked to the bike of the Samoan guy closest to him. "Ooh, look, brah, you get some dirt in da carburetor ..."

Curtis pointed to the guy's bike. The guy leaned over to check it.

Curtis kicked him full in the face.

The Samoan landed with a thud on the Civic driveway. Curtis stepped over, and his strength was enough to easily topple the guy's bike, which went down next to him.

The other Samoan took one very short, contemplative beat, then hopped on his bike and sped off down King Street.

Curtis continued on his way home, leaving the bruised and bloodied Samoan to pick up the pieces.

NEFF MAIAVA

Neff Maiava was a perfect hero for Hawaii's Samoan community. Like many local Samoans, Maiava was born in American Samoa but was brought to Hawaii when he was just an infant, so he became a true "local boy."

Because the Samoan culture had such a powerful reputation already in place for its raw physical strength, it was a very simple matter to build Neff's reputation with the fans. Maiava himself was fearless about it: He would break boards over his head, he would walk on a bed of sharp nails or he would do a Samoan fire dance with sharp knives to showcase his courage and strength.

Maiava's signature finishing move in the ring, the "coconut head butt," was his own creation. In many ways, it became the perfect symbol for our unique wrestling operation in Hawaii. Maiava's head butt was aggressive and explosive. It suggested strength at his core, in the very thickness of his skull. Above all, it was uniquely local, indigenous to Hawaii's shores.

To go with his hard head, Maiava even had hard hair. We'd play up the idea that his coarse Samoan hair was so strong it could cut into opponents' hands. We'd twist his long, wild locks into a braid and pick him up by his hair off the mat in the ring.

Stories about Maiava's courage were the stuff of legend. Wrestling lore says that, at one match on the Mainland, he was among some wrestlers who were expected to wrestle a bear. All the others refused out of fear, but Maiava was a breed apart. He carried honey with him, which he ate to give himself energy in the ring. He took his honey jar and smeared honey all over his body, then entered the ring with the bear and lay down. The fans gasped in awe as the giant bear licked Maiava, head to toe.

Whenever Maiava wrestled on the Mainland, promoters were shrewd enough to play up his "savage" image. For photographers in Canada at a press event before a big match, Maiava walked through the doors of the press room gnawing on a huge, raw fish. The flashbulbs went off from all angles as Maiava chewed away, filling the room with the distinctive aroma of raw fish. This was one savage Samoan who was certainly not blind to the value of promotion.

Outside the wrestling business, the man with the coconut head butt started his own coconut-tree-trimming business. Beyond all the wild antics in the ring, Maiava was a very resourceful, hard-working guy. At one point, Maiava was bidding to land the contract trimming all the trees on Pearl Harbor's property.

Maiava came to me to lend him some money to help secure his bid for the Pearl Harbor contract. He told me he needed $5,000 to land the bid, and that he'd pay me back. It all sounded a little fishy to me, but I was convinced I could trust Maiava, so I gave him the five grand.

Somehow the money did the trick, and Maiava and his crews got the contract to do all the trimming work at Pearl. It took a few months, but Maiava made the money back and gave me every penny he owed me. He was a very honest guy.

My business dealings with Maiava, and my respect for his character, made what happened to him later seem all the more peculiar. Toward the end of his career, but while he was still wrestling for me, Maiava was arrested on a narcotics trafficking charge. The cops claimed that Maiava had gone up to Punchbowl, and had tried to arrange some kind

of dope deal. There was also a Honolulu police sergeant arrested for his alleged involvement in the drug deal.

But Maiava was a Mormon. He didn't even drink tea or Coca-Cola, let alone mess with any kind of drugs. It was my belief—and the belief of many others—that Maiava was being railroaded for some reason.

Nevertheless, they dragged Maiava into court to try him on the drug charges. I attended the trial, in the courtroom of Judge Sam King, and the high-profile proceedings were quite a scene. Maiava's attorney had put out the request for character witnesses to testify on Maiava's behalf, so I showed up along with a few other familiar faces from the wrestling world.

At one point in the trial, the double doors to the courtroom swung open, and there stood a large-than-life character witness who'd come to testify for Maiava.

It was "Hand-some" Johnny Barend.

Johnny wasn't wrestling for me at the time—he'd left Hawaii and was working on the

Neff Maiava (right) poses with his cousin and fellow Samoan wrestling star Peter Maivia and a young fan.

65

ROGUES GALLERY

pointed at Maiava in the courtroom, and said in his distinctive voice, "Your honor, I'm here to testify for that man." He proceeded to speak eloquently about the grace and character of his fellow wrestler.

It was a bold, conspicuous act of friendship, by one member of our wrestling family on behalf of another. I was quite moved by Barend's gesture that day, and still am even now.

As a sad footnote, Maiava was convicted, I'm convinced unfairly, of the charges and served six years in the penitentiary. The Honolulu police sergeant was exonerated, and walked free.

After Maiava got out of prison, I was talking to him one day, catching up on our lives. Maiava was running a collection service in Las Vegas, and by then I was involved with my son Russ in a charter airplane service in Nevada. I was telling Maiava about our business challenges, and I happened to say, just making conversation, "Sometimes we end up chartering planes to guys who don't pay. We did that for one guy out of Las Vegas, and he owes me $11,000."

When Maiava asked who the guy was, I told him and didn't think any more about it.

Within a couple of short days, seemingly out of nowhere, the guy who owed me the 11 grand came to me and paid me in full. When he did, he said, "You know, you didn't have to send those guys around to collect. I would've paid you anyway."

I hadn't "sent" anyone. It was my old friend Maiava, looking out for family, for our Hawaii wrestling family.

RIPPER COLLINS

I think all our wrestling fans who enjoyed the matches through those glory days, from the '60s into the '70s, would have to agree that Ripper Collins was one of the most memorable, central figures in our crazy cast of characters.

Ripper was originally from Muskogee, Oklahoma—real name Roy Lee Albern—so his

Mainland. But he'd heard about Maiava's troubles, and felt he should be there. At his own expense, he made the trip.

Barend walked down the aisle in the center of the courtroom, looked Judge King in the eye, roots truly ran to the South, but, for the record, he always claimed he was from the deeper South, from Georgia.

This allowed him to wear that Southern attitude and accent on his sleeve, and completely butcher all the place names in Hawaii to completely infuriate the local fans.

Ripper would talk about a match coming up on the Outer Islands, and he'd look into the camera and say, "Well, Mr. Francis, Ah just can't TELL you how much Ah'm looking forward to seeing all our nice fans in MOW-wee and in HI-low ..." How he managed to do this with a straight face, week after week, was beyond me. It was all I could do to not crack up on camera in Ripper's company.

Somewhere along the line, Ripper acquired a sidekick named "Beauregarde." He'd actually been discovered by Neff Maiava, working out in in Dean Higuchi's gym in Hawaii when he was in the University of Hawaii ROTC program. Ripper gave him the name Beauregarde. "One name is better than two," Ripper said. "It makes you famous—like Fabian or Liberace."

(Or Velasco?)

The name stuck.

When he wrestled in Portland, Oregon, for Don Owen, Beauregarde continued to play up the "fame" angle. Every week, Beauregarde would dress up in a costume and tell the fans he was related to some other famous person, everyone from Cleopatra to Al Capone, Julius Caesar to the Pope. No one believed him. But everyone would tune in to see who Beauregarde would be related to next week.

Ripper was undeniably a great showman. But, as a pure wrestler, in the ring ... not so much. He had very little technical skill, very little natural athleticism. But that was part of his charm and mystique for the fans. This guy was heavy and getting heavier, clearly not "cut" and in shape like so many of his opponents. How could he even stand a chance in his matches?

What that meant to those of us true "shoot-ers" who wrestled a guy like Ripper—and, of course, I took on Ripper in the ring many, many times over—was a different approach, and an assortment of different ways to keep the match interesting.

If, for example, I had Ripper in a standing wrist lock, I could take him down to the mat, Ripper screaming in pain all the while. But then he could get his other hand free, reach up and yank me by the hair. A sissy move—perfectly in keeping with Ripper's personal style.

Or if I was dragging Ripper around the ring—no easy feat as he got larger and larger—he

could kick out a leg and wrap it around the ropes to get the ref's help and force me to release him. Again, a cowardly move, and one requiring no pure wrestling skill on Ripper's part. But that was Ripper.

That was why the fans would return to watch him every week. Ripper was, in many ways, Every-man: flawed, self-involved, of average athletic ability at best, but somehow resourceful enough to find ways to prevail. He was ... Homer Simpson!

One of the ways Ripper would quickly get to the fans on a regular basis was by making it all very "personal." He had a way of tossing insults about people and their families that just

The flamboyant, multi-robed Ripper Collins owed his ring fame more to showmanship than to technical skill.

made it feel and sound like dirty pool.

He loved doing it to me. Any chance he got, Ripper would begin needling me, saying derogatory things about my heritage, my upbringing in Chicago or my kids.

He began his assault on me by tracing my road back to my roots. He'd look at me with a kind of knowing glint in his eye and he'd say, "Yes, Francis. "Gentleman" Ed. From Chicago. Uh-huh. I've heard all about you."

The first time he did this, I had no idea what he was talking about. He had even me sucked in.

"What are you saying, Collins?"

"Chicago. Uh-huh. That town's all mobbed up."

This started sounding serious. What was in Ripper's twisted head?

68

"I've got some friends," Ripper would say. "Chicago friends. They told me all about you. About your ties to the … the Mafia!"

I was blindsided. Leave it to Ripper.

"You're full of it, Collins," I'd say. "You don't know what you're talking about."

"Oh, no? Don't I? Well, maybe. I'm just telling you what I heard. From my friends. Real good friends. In Chicago."

Then Ripper looked to the camera with great drama. His face was drawn in a serious snarl. "I'm having you investigated, Francis," he said, his voice dripping with vague threats. "And you can't touch me. I'm safe from guys like you, thanks to my attorneys—Sanger, Lavelle and Lavine."

Of course, anyone who took the time to look up Ripper's "legal counsel" would have a tough time locating his made-up firm anywhere on the planet.

I always knew that, at home, our fans watching the TV interviews had gotten just enough from Ripper to raise questions in their minds. Ripper was the master at that.

The reasoning of the fans would go like this:
Well, it's Ripper. He's just a fat haole.
Who can trust anything he says?
But … Maybe he does have friends in Chicago.
He comes from the Mainland.
Maybe he does know something about Ed Francis.
Is it possible that Francis is Mafia?
Maybe that's how he got to be the boss in Hawaii?

We played up Ripper's personal attacks on me to full effect. He needled me continually in the locker-room interviews, poking me again and again in the chest with that big, fat finger of his, until finally I reached a breaking point. I suggested that we settle our differences in the ring, and that, of course, led to a big main event, when I came out of wrestling retirement to take on Ripper for the Hawaii fans. He and I had a series of grudge matches that were crowd-pleasing sellouts.

I knew the rivalry between Ripper and me had our fans' full attention from what many of them would come up and say to me. After our greetings, I could tell a fan had a question he really wanted to ask me, but didn't know how. Then, with some fumbling and stammering, the fan would say to me, "Eh, Mr. Francis … Are you … Are you really in da Mafia?"

That was Ripper's gift: Give them just enough to leave them wondering.

And Ripper would keep it personal. He knew, like most folks in the Islands, that my sons Bill and Russ were high-school athletes and wrestlers—and, of course, later, both Bill and Russ joined our pro wrestling matches. But, at all stages, Ripper would look me in the eye with that sneering, arrogant scowl he wore, and he'd say, "Francis, everybody knows your sons can't wrestle. They're lousy wrestlers. No surprise, coming from a dad like you."

This kind of talk resonates with any parent in the audience. No one talks smack about your kid. It was the perfect voice to show just how low Ripper's character would go.

I made certain to react as any parent would. "Collins, you leave my family out of this," I'd growl. "There's no need for that kind of talk. One more crack about my family, you can pack your bags and get the hell off the island."

Fans would come up to me all the time and tell me not to pay Ripper any heed. They'd tell me they loved my boys, loved my family and that Ripper was a jerk.

It was my daily reaffirmation that Ripper hit them right where they lived.

But Ripper, for all his flamboyance and bravado in those locker-room interviews, had one opponent that shook him to his core: the Internal Revenue Service. Ripper simply didn't pay his taxes, so he was hounded mercilessly by the IRS.

Maybe he thought that, while he was away in Hawaii, far from the Mainland and mainstream America, he was somehow out of reach from the government's tentacles. Or maybe he simply thought the normal rules didn't apply to him. Whatever the reason, he was in some serious hot water over his taxes.

He called me asking for help. The IRS was threatening to hit him hard and shut him down. And even though I knew it was none of my business, I had to protect my investment—after all, Ripper continued to be a main-event guy for us for many years.

So I ended up working with Ripper and the IRS agent handling his case. We managed to work things out so that Ripper got off with just a couple of small penalties. It probably didn't hurt that I gave the IRS guy a few tickets to our matches, since he was a big wrestling fan. In the end, we were able to help release Ripper's bank accounts so he could pay his rent, stay in Hawaii and keep angering the fans with his continual butchering of Hawaiian place names.

HANDSOME JOHNNY BAREND

The first time I met Johnny Barend was in San Francisco. I had come to wrestle there—or so I thought. But I'd never been to a place before where they required you to have a license to wrestle. It was San Francisco's way of collecting $50 from everyone who wanted to step into the ring there.

At the time, I was pretty down on my luck, and I really didn't have an extra $50 kicking around that I could use to buy myself a license.

I was leaving the wrestling promoter's office with no license, trying to figure out what to do next, when I passed a guy going in. It was Johnny.

I didn't know it at the time, of course, but Johnny was an ex-Marine and a Korean War hero who'd brought his physical skills to the wrestling ring.

We took a moment to introduce ourselves and to talk. I told him about my predicament.

"I've never heard of a place where you need a license," I complained.

"Don't worry about it kid," Johnny said. "Here. Take this $50 for your license. You should be wrestling."

I was flabbergasted. Here was a guy who I really didn't even know, being nice to me for no reason. I thanked him.

I never forgot his kindness. As soon as I began working as a full-time promoter in Hawaii, the name Johnny Barend was at the top of my "wish list." I wanted to repay him in any way I could.

It turned out that, in truth, Johnny once again paid me, many times over. As soon as I got him over to the Islands, I discovered that, as a rising star and

crowd pleaser in Hawaii, Johnny was the complete package. Barend proved to be a promoter's dream. With that gravelly voice of his, Barend seemed to fans to always be just slightly off center, slightly on the edge.

Johnny wore knee-high wrestling boots, trademark dark glasses and a top hat, and he was seldom without a cigar. Then he adopted the TV "Batman" theme and, later, "Those Magnificent Men in Their Flying Machines," just to underscore his insanity.

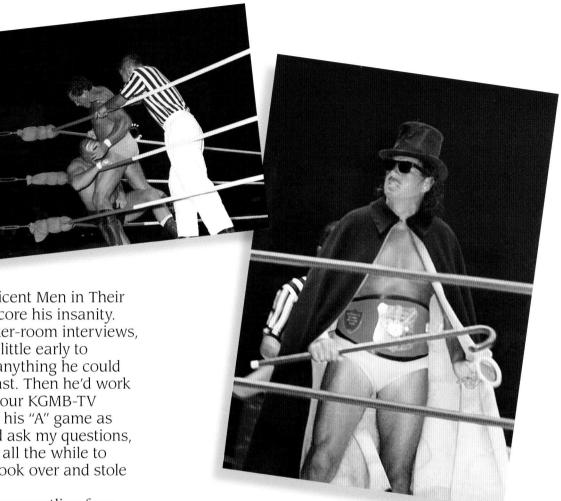

For our live in-studio locker-room interviews, Johnny would always come in a little early to scrounge around the studio for anything he could use as a "prop" during the telecast. Then he'd work out some crazy game plan with our KGMB-TV producer Phil Arnone, and bring his "A" game as soon as the red light went on. I'd ask my questions, then sit back and marvel (trying all the while to keep a straight face) as Johnny took over and stole the show.

In the hearts of our regular wrestling fans, Handsome Johnny ranked up at the top, along with Ripper, as a crowd favorite. Johnny, much like Ripper, was another true "fish out of water" for local folks, a sneering, arrogant haole. He was utterly unpredictable, capable of saying or doing anything.

I'm convinced that part of the "charm" and allure of these guys was that they were so very different than the genial, respectful people of most Island cultures. Local folks, as a rule, behaved. Johnny and Ripper, as a rule, did not.

In keeping with Johnny's "wild-child" image, he could be a bit unpredictable as an employee. Johnny's family had a business in upstate New York, and he would travel there from time to time. On one occasion, when Johnny was visiting in New York with his family, we were expecting him back in the Islands for a big main-event match we'd scheduled for him.

My phone rang, and it was Johnny. "Hey, Ed, listen," Johnny told me, with great sadness in his voice. "I'm not going to be able to make that match. My Dad passed away."

I, of course, offered my sincere condolences and told him not to worry. Family

With his trademark top hot and dark glasses, Johnny Barend was always a crowd favorite.

comes first. I told him to attend to his family's affairs in New York, and that we'd make other arrangements for the match.

A couple of weeks later, Lord Blears called the Barend family home in New York. Johnny's father answered the phone. He didn't sound so dead.

Johnny would always complain to me about the women in Hawaii. He'd come in from the beach

In September 1967 Handsome Johnny and Annie Lum wed in the ring before a sellout crowd at the HIC Arena. Opposite: The Missing Link overpowers the Magnificent Maurice.

and say to me, "What's wrong with these women here? They're all plastic! Just plastic!" I think it was Johnny's unique way of saying that the women he met were too gorgeous (and self-involved?) to give him the time of day.

Then he met one wrestling fan, a local girl named Annie Lum, out on the beach at Waikiki. They fell in love, and Johnny decided he wanted to marry her.

Not just marry her. Marry her in the ring, in a big public ceremony.

Johnny asked me if I thought that was a good idea.

I was a promoter. I needed main events, "high spots." What do you think I said?

So it was that on September 27, 1967, Johnny and Annie got married at center ring in the Honolulu International Center before a sellout crowd. Honolulu's Reverend Abraham Akaka, the pastor at Kawaiahao Church, sent one of his own clergymen to perform the service for us. As the main event that night, Curtis Iaukea took center ring just for Johnny, to wrestle ring legend Verne Gagne.

Annie became the true love of Johnny's life, inseparable from him until his passing in 2011. I've spoken with Annie since Johnny's passing, and we share countless wonderful memories of our time together with The Handsome One.

Johnny had a signature response to whatever I said, delivered in his unmistakable voice:

"Yes, yes, yes, Mr. Francis!"

It lived on long after his wrestling days in the Islands were done. When my son Russ ran for Congress in Hawaii in 2000, he and I were hosting a gathering in Honolulu. I learned that, just a few doors down, a friend of ours, Mufi Hannemann, the then-future mayor of Honolulu, was hosting another function. I dropped by to visit and, as soon as Mufi saw me, his eyes lit up. "Yes, yes, yes, Mr. Francis!" Mufi called out across the room, probably frightening and confusing many of the (younger) guests in attendance.

But Mufi knew. And I knew. Handsome Johnny Barend was in the room with us, at least for the moment.

THE MISSING LINK

Sometimes the guys we'd bring to Hawaii were positioned on the threshold, just waiting to break through as big stars for wrestling audiences. One of the guys who best fit that category was a fellow who went by the name Pampero Firpo. But Lord Blears and I would see to it that the name was going to change. So would young Mr. Firpo's life.

Firpo was pretty much of a mutt from the early going. He was an Armenian—real name Juan Kachmanian—who grew up in Argentina. He'd knocked around on Mainland wrestling circuits before we brought him over to Hawaii.

He had a great look, with wild, frizzy hair, a full beard—and he had a big personality to match his big body. But ... Pampero Firpo?

He'd apparently hatched the name as a play on the "pampas," the giant grassy plains of his Argentinian home. We knew we could do better than that.

"What should we call this guy?" I wondered aloud to Lord Blears in one of our daily plotting and scheming sessions. "He looks like some kind of wild Neanderthal. Like the missing link between ape and man."

A short beat, then Lord Blears and I looked quickly at each other, smiles on our faces. We said it in unison. "The Missing Link!"

We weren't sure Firpo would go for it. We presented it to him. "We want to call you—The Missing Link!" we said. He loved it. He said, "Ohhhh, yeahhhh!"

To add to his mystique and primitive aura, The Link had the great idea to get a shrunken head and carry it around with him. It made him all the more instantly recognizable, and it made the audience wonder: Where did it come from? Did The Link have some hand in shrinking it? What was the terrifying tale behind the tragic demise of the man who once was that head?

From a promotion standpoint, we lived for identifying gimmicks that would set the wrestlers apart and add to their reps. If anyone had told me The Link shouldn't be carrying a shrunken head around? I would have gladly told them to go bother someone else.

The Link was a wonderful guy with a huge appetite for life. That trademark saying of his— "Ohhhh, yeahhhh!"—truly characterized who he was, and just how game he was for any adventure.

(We put his picture and Ohhhh, Yeahhhh! on T-shirts, and they sold like Zippy's chili. In fact, at one point, I let my young son Sonny sell The Link T-shirts and other wrestling merchandise we offered,

73

Jim Hady looks on as the Missing Link gives autographs and accepts leis from fans.

so strong and fearless in the ring, could and would fall victim time and again to this unshakeable monkey on his back.

Link told me a story about one trip he made to Las Vegas that was truly heartbreaking. He said before leaving Hawaii on his trip, he took everything in his family's joint bank account at the time: $17,000. In those days, a handsome sum.

He checked into a hotel room in Vegas—to him, Sodom—then went down and played the slots for a while. He went back up to his room to regroup and plan the rest of his stay. That's when, he told me, he decided, "I'm going to go downstairs and get rich. I'm going to play the whole $17,000 and turn it into a true fortune!"

He gathered up his cash and headed out the door. But Link told me that, at the threshold of his hotel room door, he began to think:

I'm ruining my life.

I'm ruining my wife's life.

I'm risking everything we have.

I'm sick. I need help.

Link drew back from the doorway into his hotel room and let the door close him in. He fell onto the floor and began to weep. He took the fistfuls of money he held and threw the bills all over the hotel room. He pounded the floor and cried and cried till he couldn't cry any more.

A couple of hours went by. That's when The Missing Link, this great bear of a man who could entertain crowds by the thousands and take on any opponent in the ring, met his most powerful opponent face to face.

Slowly, carefully, he gathered up the bills that were strewn around the hotel room. He placed them in his bag. He folded his clothes back into his bag. And he took the next available flight back to his life and his wife and family in Hawaii.

through a concession at our matches. Sonny was just a kid then. When he cleared $600 profit from one night's sales, I took it away from him, gave him $50 and sunk the rest back into our operation.)

The Link's appetite had a dark side as well. Likely none of his fans knew it when he was strutting around the ring making faces at them—but The Link was a chronic, addicted gambler. As fast as he'd make money, he'd gamble it away. I never fully understood the illness that drives men to risk squandering their fortunes on games of chance, but The Link had it. Big time.

As a result, I was often cast in the role of "Father Confessor," and The Link would come to me to confess his gambling sins. He was a married man and, as he told me time and again, it of course drove his wife crazy.

It was remarkable and tragic, indeed, how this man who had such a zeal for life, and who was

ANDRE THE GIANT

For the full length of the time Andre the Giant competed in professional wrestling, he was a very big deal. Literally.

Andre was actually from France—real name Andre Rene Roussimoff—and, even though his parents and four brothers and sisters were all normal-sized people, Andre was born with a condition called acromegaly, which involves an overabundance of growth hormones.

So Andre was 6 feet 7 inches tall when he was just 17 years old. By the time I invited him to come wrestle for our Hawaii fans, Andre stood 7 feet 4 inches and weighed 500 pounds. Andre was one very big deal.

I knew he would be a huge hit with the Hawaii fans, but, just to make sure, I wanted to publicize Andre's arrival in the Islands in a big way. To get the local newspapers on board, I decided to take a series of eye-catching, provocative photos of Andre, just to showcase his immense size in visual terms that the average person could appreciate.

First, we took Andre down to a local grocery store, and took some shots of him simply pushing a shopping cart. Of course, the cart looked like some kind of tiny dollhouse toy in his massive hands. Seeing Andre in just about any everyday setting like grocery shopping was a thing to behold.

Next, we took Andre up to the top of the News Building to get a series of "superhero" shots. I figured that any true superhero would most certainly dwarf the rest of us mere mortals, so we brought along a small Japanese woman to include in the shoot.

We stood her right next to Andre on the windy platform of the roof, and the juxtaposition of the two of them was hilarious. The little woman looked like a 5-year-old child standing next to Andre. That gave me the idea to have Andre pick her up. He picked up the adult woman and cradled her in his arms like a baby.

For the final amazing photo, Andre took a ring off one of his fingers—and slipped it over the Japanese woman's wrist. Perfect fit.

The pictures were a huge hit. How could I tell? When Andre at last took to the wrestling ring for his matches, we had some of the biggest Hawaii crowds in our history.

But I needed to keep an eye on Andre in Hawaii, because I knew he had one giant Achilles heel: Andre the Giant could drink. He could drink like no one I'd ever known or seen, before or since. Because of his enormous size, Andre could easily put away more booze than five men before it had any visible effect.

On one of our outer-island road trips, I was sitting with Andre in the locker room of the arena in Hilo when a staff member delivered the "post-match snack" that Andre had ordered: a case of beer. In the span of barely over an hour, I watched as Andre had his snack. He drank every beer, one after the other, the entire case. It didn't faze him.

I witnessed this time and again when Andre and I spent a lot of time together on the Mainland, wrestling in Minnesota for then-promoter Verne Gagne and the American Wrestling Association.

One night, we headed out in a Chevy Bronco from Minneapolis for a match in Iowa, and Andre kick-started his trip in his customary fashion: with an entire bottle of brandy that he finished off before we even got to Iowa.

The matches went off without a hitch, then it was time to get back on the road. But not before a stop at a local watering hole to make some new friends and have several rounds of drinks.

Several. Rounds. of drinks.

As always, none of the rest of us could keep up as we watched Andre finish round after round after round. It always seemed that, even though Andre was pouring liquor into his throat, it must be going somewhere else from there. He just kept putting it away.

When we left the bar, Andre insisted he was

fine to drive. Honestly, I didn't doubt it. I'd seen him drink that much quite often. We piled into the Bronco and headed toward home with Andre's giant paws wrapped around the steering wheel. In almost no time I fell asleep.

I didn't sleep for long. I was suddenly jarred awake by the sound of crashing metal and a blur of darting, flashing lights. It took me an instant to realize that the flashing lights were our headlights beaming onto the spinning landscape, and the crashing sound was our Bronco rolling over and over.

I was pitched out the back window of the flipping vehicle and landed hard, face down, in the dirt. I could see the Bronco resting upside down near me. I was amazed that I'd survived the crash. But there was a powerful smell of gas, and I was afraid the car would burst into flames.

Then, after a moment of eerie silence, I heard a deep voice. "Boss, we gotta get out of here." It was Andre. He managed to climb out of the Bronco and help me to my feet. He was a bloody mess of cuts and scrapes, and I had shards of glass embedded in my head and blood dripping down my face. We were a fine pair. But we were alive.

With our car upside-down and totaled, all we could do was wait on that dark two-lane road for some help to come along. Eventually, a single car came by, and we knew we had to flag it down.

That was easy. Andre walked out in the middle of the road, waving his arms. The car stopped. Of course it did. Who's going to deny a 7-foot 4-inch, 500-pound giant, covered in blood?

It was a compact car, driven by an elderly gentleman and his wife. One look told us that there was no way we would both be able to fit in that car. Before the couple could protest, Andre scooped me up, stuffed me in their back seat, then leaned his giant mug into the old man's driver-side window and said, "Take him."

The couple took me back to the bar we'd left, and I got help from the friends we'd met to return for Andre. But I came back to find a tow truck working on our Bronco … and no sign of Andre.

Nick Bockwinkel garrotes Chief Billy White Wolf with a chain.

I had visions of my friend—the bloodied, giant beast—roaming through the night, terrorizing the countryside.

It turned out Andre had been transported by a state trooper for medical help. No charges were filed. No arrests. I never found out whether Andre's sudden off-roading while I slept was fueled by the alcohol or sheer fatigue or a combination thereof. But, somehow, we'd both survived our late-night brush with death.

We didn't quite emerge unscathed. A few weeks later, I landed in the hospital for back surgery. Later still, Andre landed at an insurance hearing, where he suddenly became very French and pretended he didn't speak English.

Who would argue with a Giant?

NICK BOCKWINKEL

Nick Bockwinkel was a fixture in our stable of wrestlers in Hawaii for many years. He came from a family history of wrestling—his dad, Warren Bockwinkel, was also a pro wrestler and got Nick into it.

Nick was an excellent combination of the two best elements in the ring—both "shooter" and "showman." He was legitimately skilled enough to really wrestle, with moves and holds that could immobilize or even incapacitate an opponent. But he also instinctively recognized the value of the "show" in show business, and he could play up his role to incite the fans, whether he was the "heel" or the "baby face" that night.

Nick was also a great family man out of the ring. He'd brought his wife and two daughters to the Islands, and our families grew close as we did things socially together. But, with Nick, sometimes that meant practical jokes … played at my expense.

Nick was an expert model-maker—he made miniature models of all sorts of planes, boats, cars, you name it. I had a 36-foot haole sampan boat that I moored at Ala Wai Yacht Harbor, and we used to take it out for boat rides and fishing trips with many of the wrestlers. One week I was called away for some wrestling business in San Francisco.

When I got back, Bockwinkel called me to say he really wanted to go out on the sampan. It seemed a little odd to me that he was so insistent about taking the boat out, but I said fine, and we agreed to meet at Ala Wai Harbor to head out.

I pulled up at the harbor, hopped out of my car and went down to the dock. But instead of my 36-foot haole sampan sitting in my assigned slip, there was an exact replica of my boat, roughly two feet long and crafted down to the finest detail, bobbing up and down in the water.

My first thought was, "Oh, my God, someone shrunk my boat!"

Then I heard the laughter behind me. There were Nick and his buddies, just waiting to see my face. While I was on the Mainland, Nick had meticulously crafted the perfect miniature version of my boat, had my real boat moved to another slip and had plopped the mini-sampan in its place. Sure, a lot of work on his part—but, if you can find ways to have a little fun in life, why not?

It's been a good, long life for Nick. While many of our "old guard" have passed on, I still talk to Bockwinkel to this day. Of course, he's a whole lot slower now, like me. The other day, when I got him on the phone, Nick said to me, "Ed, I'm sitting here naked with all these patches on me to ease the pain. My knees, my shoulders, my back ... Pretty soon I'll wear just one giant patch to cover my whole body!"

Nick and I laughed about the reality of "the golden years" for a veteran pro wrestler. Amazing memories—peppered with a whole lot of pain.

CHIEF BILLY WHITE WOLF

Some of our wrestlers built careers by carefully crafting memorable "alter egos" in the ring, and Chief Billy White Wolf was one of them. With his long American Indian headdress and "war dance," Billy had fans everywhere believing that he might have just ridden off the plains of Wyoming or the Dakotas, deep in Indian country.

The truth? Billy was born just a bit east of the American plains. Try Baghdad, Iraq.

And try putting this across the back of a wrestling robe: Billy's real Iraqi name is Adnan Bin Abdulkareem Ahmed Al-Kaissie El Farthie. Billy's dad in Iraq was a Muslim preacher, and one of Billy's high-school classmates was none other than Saddam Hussein.

Billy had been a successful amateur wrestler in Iraq before bringing his skills to the mainland U.S., where he honed his American Indian persona.

When he came to wrestle for us in Hawaii,

he'd tell me what it was like wrestling back home in Iraq. It seemed hard to believe, but Billy said the fans there were even more devoted and volatile than our U.S. fans—so much so that, with every match, there was the expectation of a riot breaking out. Billy recalled walking into the ring at the center of these rabid fans, while surrounding them were government tanks and armed guards, placed there out of necessity for safety and security reasons.

That was just for the local wrestlers. When foreign wrestlers—especially Americans—came to wrestle in Iraq, they required an armed-guard escort to and from the ring, to protect their lives.

To further complicate matters, Billy said when he returned to wrestle in Iraq after having left, the government wouldn't let him take any of his cash winnings out of the country.

Since wrestling was his livelihood, what was Billy supposed to do? He devised a plan that served his purposes. Billy would take the cash he made in the ring and buy a few cars in Iraq. He'd have them shipped stateside and, when they got to the U.S., he'd sell them to get his cash back.

Complicated? Yes, but Billy had to find innovative ways to deal with the Iraqi government.

Not long after Billy described all of this to me, he came to my office one day.

"Francis, I've got a great opportunity for a big wrestling promotion in Iraq," Billy said. "You want to go in with me on it?"

It may have been the quickest answer I ever gave in my life.

"No."

"Why not?" Billy said. "Could be huge!"

Uh, let's see. Tanks, armed guards, maybe a riot and they won't let me take the money out of the country. Have to take a pass on this one, Billy.

Billy's charisma and wrestling skill made him a big star in the Islands, and some of his biggest fans were inmates at Oahu Prison. I had already built a relationship with the inmates and the prison staff, visiting regularly to teach them wrestling moves and fitness, and one week they asked if I would bring Billy in so they could meet him.

I told them I'd be happy to bring the great Chief Billy White Wolf to meet them. I hatched a little plot for Billy's visit.

One section of the prison was dedicated to a special segment of the prison population referred to in the Islands as mahu—they were the boys-who-would-be-girls, the inmates whose sexual orientation was somewhere in between male and female. They, of course, needed their own section in the prison to avoid abuse and victimization by the general prison population.

I went to the prison coach we'd been working with, and asked if we might arrange a little "special" welcome for Chief Billy. He was happy to oblige.

Billy and I walked through the prison gates on the day of his visit and, as arranged, one of the guards offered to give Billy a little tour of the facility. He accepted graciously.

The first stop on our tour was the mahu cell block. Billy never saw it coming.

As soon as all the guy-girls got a glimpse of their handsome hero Billy, they began shrieking, squealing, cheering for him in their girly voices.

"We love you, Billy!" they cried. "Ho, you so handsome! Come here! We love you!"

They all waved at him and pressed forward, reaching out, hoping to get their

hands on this big hunk of a wrestler who'd come to visit.

Billy had that deer-in-the-headlights look on his face. He had no idea what to do.

As the guards worked to calm down all the mahus, Billy shot me an angry look.

"Francis, this is who you wanted me to meet?" he said under his breath to me.

"Hey, Chief. Our fans come in all shapes and sizes," I said with a smile.

Billy survived his special welcome, and he hung around long enough to meet many of the other inmates, shaking their hands and making their week.

The next time I invited Billy to come with me on one of our prison trips? He said no thanks.

Despite the American Indian persona that the fans all saw in the ring, Billy clung to many of his true cultural underpinnings. I'd occasionally drop by Billy's apartment in Honolulu when he was in town wrestling for us, and he invariably had a huge spread of all sorts of Middle Eastern foods laid out on the table.

We'd sit to eat, and Billy's face would light up with excitement in sharing all these delicacies with me. The overpowering smells of garlic and cumin and other unidentified spices were enough to peel the paint in Billy's tiny apartment.

"Try this!" he'd say, pointing to one bowl full of orange mush. "And this!" he'd fairly shout, pointing to a different plate of grey-green-brown blobs.

"Mmmm, fantastic!" I'd say through gritted teeth, bravely sampling each of Billy's concoctions. It was very kind of Billy to share these dishes with me. Later that evening, my stomach made sure I heard from all those dishes again.

While Billy gave me food, it turns out I gave him something he'd take around the country with him. Every time Billy came into my office, I'd give him the Hawaiian "shaka" sign. He started giving it back to me, then ended up taking it and flashing it to the fans wherever he wrestled in the mainland U.S.

Years later, when Billy was asked by a magazine writer in the Pacific Northwest where his trademark shaka sign came from, he had an easy answer.

"Oh, I got that from Gentleman Ed Francis," Chief Billy White Wolf told the writer. "He made it up."

Did I make up the shaka sign?

A little homework online suggests that it more likely may have come from the town of Laie, where a Mormon elder and expert fisherman named Hamana Kalili had the middle fingers of his right hand bitten off by an eel.

When tour drivers drove by, Hamana would wave at them from the beach with his right hand, showing only the thumb and pinkie finger remaining. And perhaps in this way the "shaka" was born.

Still … if Chief Billy White Wolf said I invented it … and he credited me in print … is there any way I might be able to get royalties every time someone flashes the shaka sign in Hawaii?

It couldn't hurt to ask, right?

GENE LEBELL

Sometimes one unusual or distinguishing characteristic would set a wrestler apart in the ring for the fans. Such was the case with Gene Lebell, whose bright red hair was an unusual sight among wrestlers.

Gene came from a wrestling pedigree. His mother, Aileen LeBell Eaton, called "The Redhead," was a very successful wrestling and boxing promoter in Los Angeles, then the only female in the business. Aileen operated out of the landmark Olympic Auditorium in Los Angeles, so Gene grew up in the company of big-name fighters like Muhammad Ali, Jerry Quarry, Joe Frazier, Sonny Liston, Sugar Ray Robinson and Archie Moore.

(In fact, Aileen was reported to have single-handedly revolutionized professional wrestling, when she told a wrestler named George Wagner to dye his hair blond and hire a valet, giving birth to the pioneering pro-wrestling superstar Gorgeous George.)

Gene had another singular talent that was not as immediately noticeable as his red hair: He was one of the foremost judo and martial arts champions in the world. He'd trained extensively in Japan in judo, karate and aikido, and he'd reportedly won some 2,000 judo matches in a row without a loss over eight years, besting a host of Olympic champions.

Gene's skill at judo seemed like an odd talent for a redhead to have, but it was one that would serve him well during his years wrestling for me in Hawaii.

As a result of his martial arts training and his devotion to fitness, Gene was a very tough guy with a powerful physique. To my delight, he was always up for all kinds of crazy stunts on TV. Once, to showcase his toughness before a match, we took a full-size motorcycle and rolled it directly over Gene's stomach. I leaned on guys like Gene with an "anything-for-the-show" attitude.

Gene was fearless. I got a call from the Honolulu Police Department to bring down some wrestlers to work with the officers in their judo and karate classes, and Gene was the first in line.

We went to the police station for their martial arts classes, and none of the cops knew that Gene, the out-of-place-looking redhead in our group, was a world-class judo expert.

The cops put up their strongest man—a big, powerful-looking Samoan—and challenged our

guys. I, of course, put up Gene. Then the cops told Gene to put on the judoji—the traditional judo jacket and pants.

Gene played the part perfectly. He took the garments and examined them, turning them over and upside down, pretending that he had no idea how to put them on. The Honolulu cops, of course, thought this was hysterical. They had no idea that the laugh was about to be on them.

Gene squared off against the big cop as we all circled around to watch. The officer locked onto Gene and showed him a few holds and moves, which Gene let him do. The cop thought he had Gene under control.

Suddenly, Gene went into a frenzy, bringing the full array of his years of judo training down on the cop's head. Bang, boom, boom—an arm bar, an uppercut, an elbow blow. Boom, boom—a stomach punch, a leg sweep and takedown. And Boom!—a crab throw and chokehold.

It was over in an instant. The big Samoan cop was flat on his back, gasping for air. The room erupted in applause—not only from all of us visiting wrestlers, but from the crowd of cops as well. They recognized the real McCoy when they saw it—even if this McCoy came with red hair.

TOSH TOGO

Some of the wrestlers who came through our 50th State Big Time Wrestling operation became very close friends of mine—and Tosh Togo was certainly one of them.

Tosh was a local boy, born on the Big Island. His real name was Toshiyuki Sakata, but when he moved to the Mainland he went by the name Harold.

Sakata was actually a skinny kid growing up. When he was 18, he weighed just 113 pounds, so he began lifting weights. Lots of young guys do it—but there was something special about Sakata. He lifted, and he lifted some more. He lifted with a vengeance.

His dedication to weightlifting paid some dividends when he stepped up on the platform to receive his silver medal in the sport at the 1948 Summer Olympics in London. That was in the light-heavyweight division. The skinny kid from Holualoa, Hawaii, had come a long way.

Sakata found his way to wrestling, and worked across the Mainland and Canada with the name Tosh Togo. By the time he came to wrestle for us in Hawaii he was a terrific draw—powerful, physically imposing and a "local boy made good."

He'd honed his skills on the Mainland, playing the "tough Asian guy" part, but, in person, he was a supremely nice guy with a "born on the Big Island" sensibility. He and I became fast friends.

When a promoter I knew from London came to visit me, and mentioned that film producers Harry Saltzman and Albert Broccoli in England were looking for an Asian man with a good body to play the part of "Odd Job" in the upcoming James Bond film *Goldfinger*, I quickly recommended Harold. I brought Harold to my office and introduced him to the London promoter, and he was impressed. He said the producers in England would pay to bring Harold to London for a screen test.

Maybe because I felt so close to Harold as a good friend, I wanted to do everything I could to help seal the deal for his audition in England. I took Harold to a local costume shop and bought him a black derby. Then we got some bricks and spray-painted them gold, and put them in an old briefcase of mine. I got some handcuffs, so Harold could handcuff the briefcase to his wrist.

I told him that, when he got to England, at the media event showcasing him for photographers, he should take the gold bricks out of the briefcase and break them apart with a karate chop. He did that.

He got the part in the movie, and his fight-to-the-death scene with Sean Connery, Agent 007, was one of the most memorable in that great film franchise's history. To this day, Toshiyuki Sakata

Big Island-born Tosh Togo found international fame when he was cast as the villain Odd Job in the James Bond film *Goldfinger*. Here, he does a job on Johnny Powers' leg in a September 1973 match in the HIC Arena.

will always be remembered as the iconic movie villain Odd Job.

When Harold came home to Hawaii after the film shoot in London, he returned with a Mercedes Benz that had a gold derby embedded in the grill, a gift to him from the *Goldfinger* producers. Harold parlayed his newfound movie stardom into a few other movie roles. He continued wrestling, but now with the new cachet of a worldwide movie star.

The last time I spoke to Harold, he was in the hospital in Hawaii. The tough kid from the Big Island, whose dedication to weightlifting took him around the globe to Olympic medals and film stardom, had been diagnosed with liver cancer. He was sure he'd beat it, like he'd conquered every other obstacle in his life. He said to me, "Ed, when I get out of here, let's go have a couple of beers."

He died four days later.

BUDDY ROGERS

If anyone asked me who in our wrestling circles was a singularly gifted athlete, the equivalent of our Michael Jordan, Peyton Manning or Wayne Gretzky, the first name that comes to mind is Buddy Rogers.

Buddy was hands-down the greatest performer in the ring I ever saw. He'd grown up in Camden, New Jersey—real name Herman Rohde—the son of German immigrants. It was very clear even in the early going that Buddy would find his way through athletics. He was, of course, a great amateur wrestler, but Buddy also boxed, played football, ran track and was a champion swimmer. There was nothing physically that Buddy couldn't do.

Watching Buddy in the ring was like watching ballet or gymnastics. He had some simply fantastic things he could do. If you were the wrestler squared off against him, some of the things Buddy could do would hurt you. But he had a way of talking you into them, whether it was going over the top ropes, or taking Buddy's full weight flying into your chest. Buddy had the athletic skill to make it happen, and you went along for the ride.

That's why it was such an honor for me to be in a position as promoter to bring a guy like Buddy to perform for local Hawaii fans. I knew that, with Buddy, they would be treated to feats of agility they had never seen before, and would likely never see again in their lifetimes.

Step into the ring with me for a moment, for a typical match with the great Buddy Rogers.

Buddy has me in a headlock and is working me over. I take him and throw him hard toward the ropes. Buddy flies across the ring, with his blond hair trailing wildly behind him. He rebounds off the ropes, and I set myself to drop-kick him hard.

I take my best shot. But I miss badly, because somehow Buddy has managed to grab the ropes and skid to a dead stop, clear of me, leaving him free to strut around the ring unharmed. He has once again defied the laws of physics in the ring, and the fans go absolutely berserk.

As testament to Buddy Rogers' incomparable athletic skill—and durability—Buddy spent his life defending his standing as the one true "Nature Boy" in wrestling history. He'd come by the billing due to his natural gifts, of course, his innate athletic prowess and skill.

So whenever another Nature Boy would come along, a pretender to his title, Buddy would rise to the occasion. Later in his career, Buddy wrestled "Nature Boy" Ric Flair in 1978, when Ric was a rising star in the WWF and Buddy was 57 years old. Buddy was set to wrestle yet another new Nature Boy, Buddy Landel, in 1992 … when Buddy Rogers was 71 years old.

But Buddy Rogers passed away later that year. Till the very end, he'd pursued what he loved, and had performed it better than anyone could.

FREDDIE BLASSIE

Freddie Blassie was a huge star in Los Angeles, wrestling for promoter Jules Strongbow. He was also a recognizable name in many wrestling venues across the Mainland, particularly his home turf of St. Louis and in Georgia and the Southeast.

Blassie was a great "heel." Word was that Blassie was so hated in Southern

Ed gets the worst of it against Freddie Blassie, the consummate "heel," whose specialty was biting opponents.

California that he required a police escort to and from L.A.'s Olympic Auditorium, just so he'd survive all the crazy fans who wished him harm.

In fact, in one match against none other than my partner Lord Tally Ho Blears, a fan threw acid on Blassie's back. He had to immediately stop the match to hurry out and wash it off.

I felt very lucky to work it out for him to come appear before our Hawaii fans. To our local fans he was another arrogant Mainland haole, cut out of a similar mold as Ripper Collins or Johnny Barend. When he showed up to wrestle on our cards, he already had his patented trademark saying well in place.

Blassie would get a lot of mileage calling his opponent—any opponent—a "pencil-neck geek." It was a cutline our fans hadn't heard before Freddie, and it stuck with them.

The costumes, the attitudes, the trademark sayings of the wrestlers—they were all like a comfortable shoe for our audiences, or the refrain of a favorite song. You return to it because you feel comfort in the familiar. Fans would tune in to our TV show, or come to our matches in person, and just wait for Freddie to call someone a "pencil-neck geek."

He was always more than happy to oblige.

Just to show how tough he was (at least in the eyes of our crowd), Blassie would wait till the TV cameras were rolling for our locker-room show or the matches at the Civic. Then he'd produce a metal file and, while the cameras were rolling, he'd start filing his teeth.

He'd boast about how he wanted his teeth nice and sharp so he could bite his opponent. But I never saw Blassie bite anyone. He never really explained why he didn't—but then, he didn't have to. He was the great "Classy Freddie Blassie." If he felt like filing his teeth, just for sport, no one would argue with him.

I always wondered what Blassie's dentist might say when he showed up for an appointment. Did his dentist tell Freddie it wasn't good to take a rasping metal file to your teeth? Or was he just happy to take Freddie's money, to pay for his house on the beach and his expensive car? I'm sure after all the filing, Blassie's dental bills were more than chump change.

GIANT BABA

I met Giant Baba in Japan when he was wrestling for promoter and legendary Japanese wrestling superstar Rikidozan. Baba had first played pro baseball in Japan, but, at 6 foot 10 inches tall, Baba was always kind of a "freak of nature" there, and it was almost inevitable that he'd find his way to the wrestling ring.

85

To the delight of the fans, Curtis Iaukea uses a stool against Giant Baba at ringside. Below: Baba celebrates a victory. Opposite: Luther Lindsay (left) and Neff Maiava leave the ring after a match.

But when I went over to Japan on wrestling business, it was odd to see the way Rikidozan treated Giant Baba. Riki would position Baba at his door, more like a security guard or slave to him. We might be inside, having a

meeting over which of my wrestlers Riki would like to bring to Japan, and which of Riki's wrestlers were suitable for my Hawaii fans.

Then it would be time to order in some food from a restaurant. Riki would get up, go to the door where Baba was positioned "on duty"—give him our food order and slap him hard in the head. I was stunned and taken aback by this treatment—especially given Baba's truly giant stature and imposing figure.

But it was simply the culture there. Riki was the boss. He was a legend who'd begun in the sumo ranks, then became a hero to Japanese fans by defeating an endless succession of American wrestlers in the years after World War II, when their country had been soundly defeated by America. Riki was "the man." Baba was a willing servant.

Beyond that, the practice of hitting or punching to establish authority was a fixture in the very fabric of the Japanese culture. It was standard operating procedure at, for example, the Etajima Naval Academy, where, if an underclassman failed to properly salute a senior cadet, he would be punched five times in the face. So, though I was shocked at Baba's treatment at the hands of Rikidozan, it was not unusual in that environment.

LUTHER LINDSAY

Luther was a great shooter in the ring. He was a top-ranked amateur wrestler and went on to play football in the Canadian Football League. For our operation in Hawaii, Luther stood out because he was one of the few African Americans our fans saw compete.

I travelled with Luther when we wrestled on the Mainland. When we worked in towns around the South, they still had segregated water fountains,

I eventually said to him, "Luther, doesn't it bother you to be treated this way?"

"No, forget about it," Luther said. "It's just normal to me." Despite his enormous physical power, he'd found a way to make his peace with the injustice he faced on a daily basis.

But even Luther had a breaking point. At one of our matches in Hawaii, Luther was in the ring in the middle of a tough fight when a fan began to yell out, "Get da popolo!"

Luther knew very well what popolo meant. Especially used in that context. He turned and spotted the angry fan, then left his business in the ring behind him. Luther went through the ropes and into the crowd and grabbed the guy who'd been yelling. I knew I had to protect Luther from himself. I sent the ref out to break it up and stop the match.

Of course, I didn't want anyone to get hurt. But I have to admit: After what I'd seen Luther subjected to in the deep South, it made me quietly happy to see that he wasn't willing to accept more intolerance in a place like Hawaii.

HARD-BOILED HAGGERTY

Haggerty was one very tough guy from Southern California, real name Don Stansauk. Out of the University of Denver he went to the NFL, where he played for the Detroit Lions and the Green Bay Packers before entering the pro wrestling ranks.

In fact, the first time I ever met Haggerty was early on, when I was first wrestling for promoter Karl Pojello. Haggerty walked into the wrestling locker room with some of his Green Bay Packer teammates, all in their Packers sweaters. They'd just dropped by to meet the wrestlers. Then, within a couple of years, I ended up helping train Haggerty in Ohio to become a professional wrestler after his football days were over.

Maybe because he had to be tough on the football field, by the time Haggerty came to wrestle for me in Hawaii he'd already cemented his angry,

toilets, restaurants and other things. It made me furious, because Luther was a close friend, and we'd find ourselves in situations where the management would literally separate us in order to make Luther obey the segregation laws.

We'd approach some restaurant and Luther would glance in the window, then tell me, "I can't go in there." So I'd go in and talk to the management, explaining that he was a fellow wrestler, a colleague, a friend.

They might then let Luther in the back door of the restaurant, where Luther would be required to go take a seat in the kitchen. I'd follow him, go into the kitchen and we'd have our meal there. Together.

ROGUES GALLERY

Left to right: Freddie Blassie, Hard-Boiled Haggerty and Ripper Collins use Civic Auditorium folding chairs as weapons in a tag team match that strays outside the ring.

tough around the Civic—there were just a few spaces in the front of the arena, and for some reason they were reserved for taxis.

As luck would have it, just as Haggerty was pulling in, a taxi cab pulled in at the same time. There was only one available parking space.

The cab driver stepped on the gas and zoomed into the space ahead of Haggerty. Haggerty pulled in right behind him and stopped.

When the cab driver got out of his taxi, Haggerty got out and walked over to him, just to politely "discuss" the parking situation.

But the cabbie was a big guy and didn't want to hear anything from Haggerty. He found some very creative names to throw at my wrestler.

Bad idea.

Remember: This is a guy who came out of the NFL, and now made his living throwing great big men around a little ring.

Haggerty stepped up to the cab driver, put his giant paws on the guy's chest and yanked. The entire front of the cab driver's aloha shirt ripped off like the last sheet of toilet paper on a roll.

As the cabbie stood stunned, Haggerty patiently took the time to "explain" the situation to him.

"I'm a professional wrestler," Haggerty said, "so I can't hit you. But here's what I can do. And what I'm going to do."

Haggerty pointed to the pay phone in front of the Civic. "I'm going to go use that phone and call some of my friends who aren't professional wrestlers. They won't have any problem hitting you."

Haggerty stepped over the curb fronting the arena. "My friends will come over, and they'll bring you to this curb, and they'll put your leg on the curb, and they'll stomp on your leg and break it. Just wait here."

With that, Haggerty walked to the phone to place his call. Or at least, to pretend he was calling.

The cab driver came running into the Civic and found me in my office. He was scared. He was

tough-guy character in the ring. Out of the ring, he was a crazy, hard-living, unpredictable guy, always full of surprises for me and sometimes a little tough to handle.

On occasion, a little of that hard-boiled anger would leak over into his real life. There was a day at the Civic when Haggerty drove up in his old beater car. Parking was always

88

angry. And what was left of his aloha shirt was hanging off him in shreds.

"Your wrestler did this to me!" the cabbie screamed. "And … and he threatened me!"

"All right, now, calm down," I said, in the most soothing voice I could muster. "Yeah, that Haggerty, he's a very high-strung guy. Even I can't control him most of the time."

I walked over to my cash drawer and pulled out a thick wad of singles. As the cab driver watched, I began counting out dollar bills in front of him. One, two, three, four …

The cab driver's shirt was maybe worth eight dollars. When I got to around 20 I said, "I'm really going to get on Haggerty, try to get him under control. It's just not safe when he gets so crazy."

Twenty-one, 22, 23 …

When I got to 40 I stopped, and handed him the bills. "Haggerty pulls anything like this again, I'm going to ship him out of Hawaii."

"Well … Okay, Mr. Francis," the cabbie said. He took the bills, folded them into his aloha shirt pocket—which was now hanging down somewhere around his waist—went out to his cab and left.

Haggerty took his parking space. ♦

Blood sport: Injuries—sometimes serious—are a way of life for professional wrestlers. Opposite: In a hugely hyped fight in Texas, Ed wrestled the great international champion Lou Thesz to a draw, despite head injuries from a metal chair thrown by a fan the previous night.

CHAPTER 10

The Scars Are Real

sk any of our great wrestlers who took the ring in Hawaii.

The number one line of questioning we would always get, in Hawaii and around the country, even from our most loyal and avid fans was: Isn't it all fake? Isn't it just a big, phony show?

My answer involves looking at some of the things my wrestling colleagues and I went through in the ring on a daily basis. After looking at the real life of a working professional wrestler, you tell me whether you think it's all a big put-on.

Let's start with a typical day for a pro wrestler. On most days when I was wrestling around the country, my evening's match might have been 200 to 300 miles away from my home base. I'd pack my bag and hit the road, trying to time it so that I'd arrive at the arena a couple of hours before the show.

As a "star" when I was the World Junior Heavyweight Champ, I had some big responsibilities. Promoters and wrestlers alike depended on me to draw a large crowd, so that we could all have a good payday. I, of course, needed to leave the arena with the least amount of damage to my reputation and to my body. You get hurt, you're done.

The promoter had his own agenda. Even if I was destined as the "champ" to win the match, the promoter might want to make sure that his

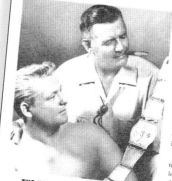

Here's Why We'll Beat Thesz!

"Francis The New Champ"
says Al Ventres

"As manager of the present champion of Texas and the next champion of the world, I am taking this opportunity to tell you fans that we will positively beat Louis Thesz when we meet him here next week."

"I have had some difficulty explaining to you over the microphone that Francis is the greatest wrestler I have ever seen, therefore I am spending my own money taking my own time to get this important message across to you . . . namely . . . that Gentleman Edmund Francis will be the next champion of the world after he meets Louis Thesz next week."

"This is not idle talk, although I admit that I sometimes talk a little too much. But I have been in wrestling for a great many years and I have never seen a man with the ability, the physique, the courage, the know how and the willingness of Gentleman Ed."

THE WORLD'S GREATEST MANAGER and THE WORLD'S GREATEST WRESTLER

"In addition to that he is fortunate in having the greatest manager in the world. I searched for four years to find a man of Ed's calibre and I have trained him to the minute for the chance at the title. He will not let me down."

"I admit Thesz has a good manager too. But I was the middleweight champion of the world and Lewis was the heavyweight champion. We middleweights always had to know more wrestling than the big clumsy fellows like Lewis who depended on their size and weight to win for them. I have taught Gentleman Ed all of these tricks and they will win for us against any combination of men."

"You people know his ability, you have seen him win match after match, you have seen him take the Texas title and hold it despite the underhanded methods of his opponents, the unfair use of flowers to try to irritate his allergy and make him sneeze, and many other dirty, sly, nasty methods that have failed because this boy really has the goods."

"Ed Francis is young. Lou Thesz is at the end of the trail, an old man of 35. He will feel his years next week when the spirited youth of my boy takes charge of the match."

"Thesz does not really have experience, he relies too much on Ed Lewis, but next week he will be outsmarted in his corner too and we will whip him."

"I intend to keep the Texas state title belt as a souvenir when we win the world's title belt next week. I personally put up a belt that will go to some lesser light who will travel in Gentleman Ed's footsteps. I will title belt we will take on a grand tour of the Orient, the Pacific and Europe. We will wrestle before the crowned heads of Europe and prove that we are truly champion of the world."

"Next week will prove that we have the ability and also prove my statement that Lou Thesz is through!"

"And now, Gentleman Ed Francis, the next world's champion, will be only too glad to autograph this for you as a momento of this occasion."

With the game plan set and the prelims over, it's time to enter the ring. Our ring was like concrete with a thin matte cover. The rings we wrestled in had no springs like they do now to absorb the shock of a body slam, and the matte cover was a disgusting patchwork of filth. There was resin, sweat and blood that saturated the cover, left over from the previous week's boxing matches, a perfect breeding ground for bacteria.

As a result, many wrestlers contracted an eye disease called trachoma, and some would even lose their eyesight from it. Years on the horribly unsanitary mats for Strangler Ed White and Cowboy Luttrell left them both legally blind. Luttrell ultimately ran the promotion in Florida and, whenever I visited his office, he and Ed White would be playing cards. White had to hold the cards an inch from his nose to be able to see them.

Next on the agenda for the night: time to give the fans some excitement. The title of "champ" didn't mean I was the good guy. On the contrary, most of the time I was the heel—the villain.

I enter the ring, strut around and maybe give a defiant finger to the crowd. My posturing triggers 5,000, maybe even 10,000 angry fans to start screaming: "Kill the bastard!" "Tear his head off!" "Put a hurt on him!" And, of course, many other things not remotely fit for print.

The bell rings and the match is underway. It's a one-fall, 60-minute time limit.

For maybe the first 25 or 30 minutes, my opponent is getting the best of me. The fans are happy, screaming their approval. But then the tide turns. I get a headlock on my opponent and start punching him in the head. He might secretly produce a razor blade that he's had hidden in his wrist band, or even in his mouth, and he privately uses it on his forehead. Now blood is running down his face. The fans are going wild.

I turn away from the referee, reach into my trunks and pull out my brass knuckles. I hit my bloodied opponent again, then put the brass knuckles

Billed as the Sicilian Stretcher Death Match, this bloody battle between Pedro Morales and Johnny Barend, staged in the HIC Arena in March 1970, ended with an unconscious Barend carried from the arena on the stretcher. Opposite: On Christmas 1969 at the HIC, badly bloodied wrestler Hahn Lee appears in street clothes, claiming he'd been mugged in the locker room by Ripper Collins and Friday Allman. The match between Pedro Morales and Johnny Barend is temporarily halted as Morales and Nolan Rodrigues escort Hahn from the ring.

guy wouldn't be made to look foolish in the process. After all, his guy is the "baby face" and the local big shot in that territory. You have to leave him with his dignity.

In planning our "high spots" for a match with my opponent—often a complete stranger—I'd try to lay down a few very simple ground rules. The primary one: no pile drivers. You can't trust a guy with your spinal cord, especially when you never know if his ego could suddenly cause him to go rogue on the champ.

back inside my trunks. The fans see what I've done and their yelling builds to a crescendo of boos.

As the match draws to a conclusion, the promoter has assembled the evening's other wrestlers outside the locker room. They know the drill, all too well. They have to be ready to run down to protect me when the match is over.

Meanwhile, in the ring, for the final punctuation point to the match, I pick up my opponent, slam him to the mat and cover him. One, two, three! I jump up and raise my hand in victory.

The fans, who just spent the past hour going hoarse rooting for the other guy, all go crazy with anger. On more nights than I can count, some fans would jump up on the ring apron, trying to get at me. I would end up having to punch some of them off the apron just to protect myself.

That's when the other wrestlers run to ringside to help protect me. Together we fight our way back to the locker room, shoving, pushing, swinging and punching through the sea of angry fans who have closed around us.

At a match in Toronto, I was running to get to the relative safety of the locker room, but the crowd was right on top of me. I knew they'd be able to trap me before I'd made it to safety, so I had to do something drastic. I whipped around and hit the first face in the crowd, the one closest to me.

The fan dropped like a sack of rice.

When he went down, it distracted the crowd just long enough for me to slip into the locker room. But the fans weren't going to give up and go away that easily. They started pounding on the locker room door, trying to break it down to get at me.

Now I was mad.

I swung open the door and pulled one of the fans inside. We swung at each other, and I hit him so hard I broke his jaw. How do I know? The next week, the same guy was right back at the matches … with his jaw wired shut.

It was all in a night's work for a working wrestler.

THE SCARS ARE REAL

And remember: That was just one night's work, in a week that would include five or six more nights just like it. After a few moments in the locker room, to cool off and make sure I didn't have any injuries that required medical attention, I'd still have that 200 to 300 miles to drive home before I could sleep.

For my services rendered in and out of the ring, how am I physically compensated? I had far too many broken ribs to count. I also lost count long ago as to the exact number of times I've had my nose broken—especially because many of those times I asked my opponent to make it happen.

If things were slow in a particular match we were in, and I wanted a "high spot" to get the fans excited, I'd lean in to my opponent and whisper, "Get me in a headlock and punch me in the nose."

The usual response was, "Are you nuts?" But I knew how fragile the nose area was, and what the result would be. "No, no, go ahead, it's all right," I'd tell my opponent. As soon as he accommodated my request and bopped me hard across the bridge of my nose, the blood would start gushing and the fans would go wild.

In the heat of battle, it really didn't even hurt that much.

Okay, it hurt.

But it wasn't anything I couldn't handle and, at the end of the day, our job was to put on a good show for the fans. If a little blood helped the show along, could anyone really blame me?

Some of my blood loss in the wrestling arena was by no request of mine. At a match in a small town in Texas, some fans were incensed about the way I'd pinned their local baby-face star. (All right, I may have held his trunks just a bit outside the view of the ref.) The arena's metal folding chairs started to fly, and though I dodged most of them, one caught me square on top of my head. Blood shot out everywhere.

My manager then, a guy named Al Ventres, rushed me to a doctor, who sewed me up and gave me a tetanus shot for safety. But the very next day I was scheduled to wrestle the great Lou Thesz in Houston, in a hugely hyped match for the new International Heavyweight Championship belt. I awoke to discover a thick red rash across my back. It was an adverse reaction to the tetanus shot I'd received.

It got worse.

When I looked in the mirror, I could barely see my face behind the enormous mass of flesh hanging over my eyes. It was a giant flap of scalp, swollen grotesquely from the point where the chair had hit me in the head the night before.

But the show must go on, right?

Back to the emergency room I went, for a shot to counteract the tetanus reaction. It instantly made me feel better, but as I got up from the gurney I passed out and fell to the ER floor. I rallied as best I could and, though I was weak as hell, the swelling went down and I answered the opening bell that night in Houston. I wrestled Thesz to a draw for the International Heavyweight Championship.

Another match I had with Thesz in Calgary, Canada, turned out to be unforgettable, for all the wrong reasons. Lou drop-kicked me in the forehead, and I was supposed to fly backward over the top ropes onto the floor of the arena.

It all went according to plan, with one small kink.

I had taken a razor blade that was taped inside my trunks and had put it in my mouth for safekeeping. Turned out, not so safe. When I flew over the ropes, the blade flew out of my mouth and onto the floor. I scrambled to grab it so the fans wouldn't see it. I was supposed to use it to give myself a scratch on the forehead, to add just a dash of blood to the proceedings.

But in the hustle and confusion over grabbing the exposed blade, I inadvertently cut too deeply into my forehead and hit an artery. Blood started literally shooting out like a geyser. The bleeding got so bad that the ref had no choice but to stop the

match and count me out. The emergency staff on hand managed to quickly suture the cut with tape to stop the flow and allow me to make it home.

When I got home, I pulled off the tape to survey the damage. Big mistake. Blood again shot out, splashing onto the mirror like something out of a horror film. I wrapped a towel around my head, called 9-1-1 and an emergency team got me through a snowstorm to the hospital for 10 stitches.

Through the years my list of injuries goes on and on. One night, I took a karate chop to the throat that did so much damage I was on only liquid foods for weeks, and still have the gravelly voice to show for it. I had both hips replaced. And I had a severely dislocated shoulder that plagued me for the length of my career.

It began when I was wrestling in Philadelphia, in the main event against a great big guy with a big belly. I don't remember his name—perhaps I've repressed it on purpose. In the middle of the match, I grabbed the guy's arms, threw him into the corner and rushed at him. The idea was to slam into his big belly, but grab onto the ropes on either side of him so as not to hit him too hard.

Opposite: One of the more lethal weapons employed during an HIC wrestling match was this folding table hauled up into the ring from the arena floor.

But his stomach was so big that my arms never made it to the ropes. When I hit him with such force, it immediately dislocated my left shoulder. I could instantly feel as my shoulder popped out and slipped down under my pectoral muscle.

At the next possible break in the action, the inept commission doctor in the arena had some wrestlers hold me down, and he tried yanking on my arm to pop my shoulder back in its socket. I was certain I was going to black out from the pain, and what the doctor was doing wasn't working at all.

They took me to the hospital, where an orthopedic doctor used a fluoroscope to examine

THE SCARS ARE REAL

the shoulder, then twisted my arm to get my shoulder realigned.

I literally spent the rest of my career protecting the shoulder, because the wrong move would throw the shoulder out again. At least half a dozen times I recall it popping out during a match. But I remembered what the orthopedist had done to realign it, so I'd hold the ring ropes and pop it back in myself like it was all part of the action.

One night in Canada, that shoulder injury came back to bite me. I was wrestling in a tag-team match, partnered with a great wrestler named Vic Christie. Some unruly fans had gotten to Vic during the match, punching and kicking him when he was out of the ring.

One of the fans in particular was really giving it to Vic, and I thought, "I'm gonna get this SOB." I grabbed the ring ropes to climb up and jump on the fan. But as I swung out from the ropes I felt that all-too-familiar *pop!* It was the damn left shoulder, now dead weight.

I landed in front of the brawling fan, hunkered down beneath him, now just trying to protect my incapacitated left side with my right arm. The fan saw his opportunity. He gave me a swift kick that caught me full under my chin, splitting it wide open. I'm bearing the scar there today, of that night

in Canada when my bum shoulder once again let me down.

I had an endless succession of back injuries and bulging discs, attended to by chiropractors in every city in the U.S. Those back problems ultimately resulted in two major surgeries.

Many nights when I was wrestling I'd lie on a wood bench in the locker room to try to get a little relief from the searing pain in my back. Then I'd hear them call my name for the main event that night. I'd take a deep breath and struggle to pull myself off the bench and into a standing position. I'd gingerly pull on my jacket, or whatever I was wearing that night into the ring, and I'd slowly head out the locker room door into the arena.

But every night that I crossed the threshold of that door and into the arena, something strange would happen. The people were all on their feet, screaming for the match to begin, screaming my name. I could see all their faces.

It was at that moment, when my face met the fans, that I straightened up, walked into the ring and the pain disappeared. I went the distance in the match, gave the fans their money's worth, then went back to the locker room and into the shower, and the pain came flooding back, coursing through my spine.

Call it "fan adrenalin," call it mind tricks, call it a crazy way to make a living—but, somehow, some way, the sheer will to perform for me and all the wrestlers led us to conquer the pain at least temporarily, long enough for us to survive our minutes in the ring.

Believe it or not, with all the pain I experienced, I'm one of the lucky ones. The physical toll that the sport of wrestling took on all the competitors was relentless.

The great wrestler Fred Blassie wrestled through the pain with serious kidney problems. When the pain got to be too much, Blassie finally went to the hospital, where doctors told him they wanted to remove one of his kidneys. Blassie called me looking for some advice, so I headed down to the hospital to be with him.

When I walked into his hospital room, Blassie was in such pain that he was up out of bed, jumping and writhing around the room, screaming in agony. I called for the doctors to give him some kind of injection or painkiller to give the poor guy a little relief from the pain.

They took Blassie into surgery and removed one of his kidneys. It was a safe bet that his troubles were either brought on, or at least made worse, by years and years of brutal abuse to his internal organs inside the ropes.

The Samoan wrestler Peter Maivia—superstar Neff Maiava's cousin—was similarly afflicted with kidney problems. Doctors also went in and removed one of Peter's kidneys. Even though the medical care at that time could not definitively tell if the wrestlers' kidney problems were a direct result of being punched and kicked in the ring, with both Blassie and Maiava I felt a huge sense of responsibility for their situations, and I footed all the medical bills for their surgeries and recoveries.

So ... pro wrestling's all fake?
Ask Maivia. Ask Blassie. Ask their doctors.
Or ask Sonny Myers.
Myers was a wrestling friend of mine, a tough shooter originally from Missouri. One night at our match in Waco, Texas, things got way out of control. Sonny was trying to get out of the ring and away from the crazed mob when two guys grabbed him and held him. Another fan pulled out a long, curved linoleum knife and sliced Sonny across his belly, right through his wrestling trunks.

Sonny's intestines spilled out into his hands.

It was an absolute miracle that the knife wound didn't cut into Sonny's intestines. We rushed him to the ER—still holding his intestines—and the doctor was able to sew him up. Sonny was back in the ring wrestling within a few months. (In fact, Sonny had a long career in wrestling, and went on to train a host of young wrestlers, among them Hulk Hogan.)

Fake? Ask a couple of wrestlers named Yukon Eric and Killer Kowalski.

In the waning moments of a big match between the two of them, I was watching as Killer slammed Eric near the corner of the ring. Then Killer climbed up on the top ropes for the big finale. He leapt off the ropes, with the intent of appearing to land on Eric's throat.

But Killer missed his mark. Kowalski's knee accidentally swiped the side of Eric's head with such immense force that it popped Eric's ear clean off. I watched, awestruck, as the ref grabbed the ear and put it in his pocket.

Eric was rushed to the hospital, but the ear could not be reattached.

(One sad footnote: Yukon Eric's life ended tragically. Some years later, Eric returned home from a wrestling road trip to find that his wife had left him, and had taken all the furniture. He was despondent. Yukon Eric drove to his church, parked his car, put a gun to his head and shot himself dead.)

So. Pro wrestling. All a big, phony show? Just silly, light entertainment? No consequences? All a big fake?

You tell me. ◆

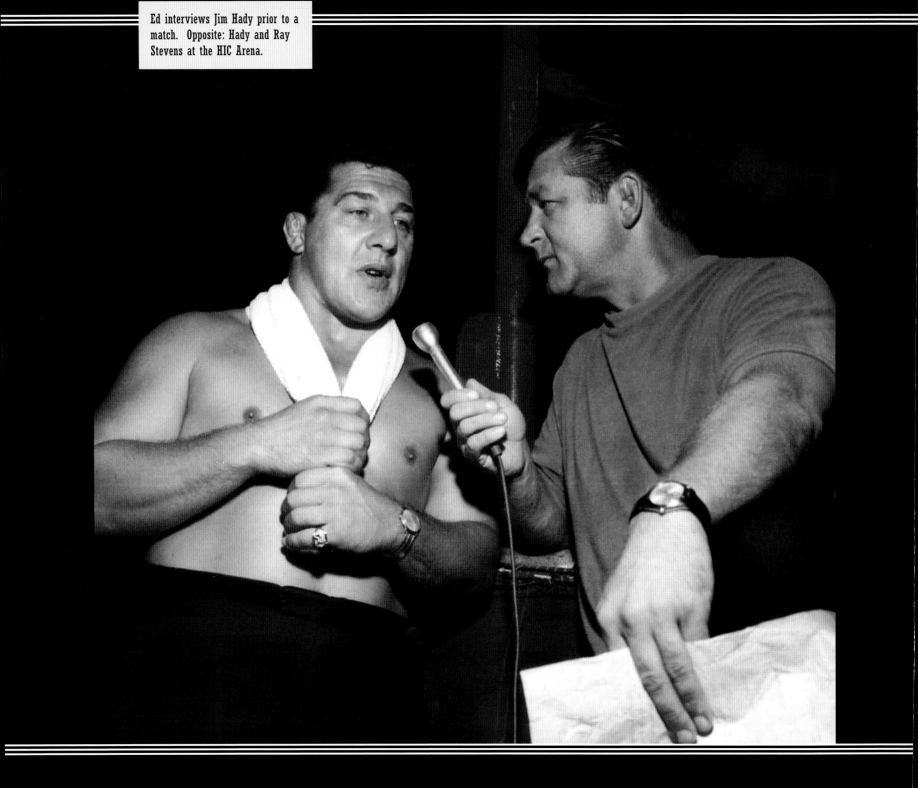

Ed interviews Jim Hady prior to a match. Opposite: Hady and Ray Stevens at the HIC Arena.

CHAPTER 11

Requiem for a Friend

Every wrestler I knew, every wrestler I fought, every wrestler I spoke with in the years following our battles felt the residual aches and pains of combat.

But the greatest personal pain I ever felt connected with the sport of wrestling was not a physical pain at all. It was a shocking, unexpected tragedy that haunts me to this day.

The events of that terrible night—seared in my memory today—began at one of our regular matches out at Conroy Bowl at Schofield Barracks.

The main event that night was a tag-team match featuring Lord Blears paired with a fine wrestler named Jim Hady, going up against the dastardly duo, Ripper Collins and Johnny Barend.

Hady and I had been close friends. He was a good, solid shooter, very well-schooled in the ring, and I booked him often.

Beyond that, I did more things socially with Hady than with any other wrestler. For much of the time I was in Hawaii, I owned a boat, and Hady and I would go out fishing and diving. He was a great friend to spend time with, a really nice guy and a true gentleman.

At Schofield Barracks on that night—January 13, 1969—I was worn out. On any other night, I would have stayed until the final bell, but on that night it had been a tough week and I was exhausted. I went through the money receipts and took care

of the business side, then I went home early, leaving it to some of the other guys to wrap up for the night when the matches were over.

Shortly after I got home, my phone rang. It seemed strange, given the lateness of the hour, and, as with any late-at-night call, you immediately have concerns. A pall began to fall over the night for me.

The phone call was from Hady's wife. I could instantly hear the alarm in her voice. She said after Hady got home, he just sat in a chair and would not respond to her.

Hady's wife tried to laugh, nervously. She said that sometimes Jim would do that as a joke, but then he'd pop open his eyes and laugh at her for

99

REQUIEM FOR A FRIEND

getting worried. This time, though, she said it didn't look like he was kidding. I could hear her voice cracking.

I said to her, "Tell Jim I'm on the phone. I want to talk to him."

His wife went to him, then came back to the phone. She said Jim didn't respond. I called 9-1-1 right away.

An ambulance rushed to Hady's house, and the paramedics called to tell me they were taking him to St. Francis Hospital. They gave me few details about his condition, but I knew it was serious. I prepared to head out to St. Francis.

But another phone call from the paramedics let me know that they had stopped at an emergency clinic on the way to the hospital. I feared the worst.

In moments, I got the word. "We're very sorry, Mr. Francis. They pronounced Jim Hady dead at the clinic."

The words hit me like a wrecking ball.

I had been with this man hours earlier, laughing and joking with my good friend, the strong, strapping wrestler. This could not be happening. Hady was just 38 years old. A friend. A husband. Father of a young daughter.

They brought Jim Hady's body to St. Francis. They asked me to go to the hospital to officially identify the body.

I walked into the morgue and they pulled the covers back. The first thing that caught my eye was the Catholic cross on a chain that Hady wore around his neck. They hadn't removed it yet, and it gleamed in the harsh light of the morgue.

My next impression was that, somehow, in some strange way, Hady had shrunk. He was always such an animated, imposing, robust figure in the ring and in life. Now, in death, it felt to my eye like he was just half the size of the man I'd known. Something had left his body, some power, some force. I wanted to believe it was his enduring soul that had moved on.

The room was dead silent. There was an antiseptic smell. Gazing on my close friend lying in repose, I thought about the great times we'd had together, and about the tremendous performances Hady had given fans in the ring.

I can't tell you how long I stood there, as Hady lay motionless before me. I paid my silent respects to Jim and to his family. I thought about all the great wrestlers who came before him, and those who would follow, who gave so much to their fans in the name of the sport they loved.

Those moments in the morgue, seeing Hady lying with eyes closed, opened mine. I saw in an instant that, while we were busy every day making a show for the fans, we never confronted our own mortality. Wrestling is a loud, explosive, violent undertaking. But the finality and utter silence of death is a world apart, a different mindset altogether.

I asked the attending medical personnel to take Hady's cross and a ring that he was wearing, and to make sure his wife received them. Then I went to sit for some time with her and their young daughter. They were in a waiting room in the hospital upstairs. I made sure that some people would get them safely home that night.

The next day, to add real insult to the loss we were all feeling, a local Honolulu radio DJ made light of Jim's passing. The jock said that Jim was

probably not dead at all, and that it was likely just some phony wrestling stunt cooked up by promoter Ed Francis. That hurt.

The following week, we held a memorial service for Jim at the matches at the Civic. I gave all the proceeds from the matches to Jim's widow. At the conclusion of those matches, I had the timekeeper ring the bell 10 times, slowly and solemnly, in honor of Jim's passing. It meant a great deal to me.

The service had an odd effect on the fans. After it, many of our core fans stayed away from the matches for the next month. Perhaps the reality of Hady's death intruded on the pure escapism of wrestling they so enjoyed.

I could understand how affecting it was for the fans. Other than his family, there was no one more affected by Hady's death than I was.

When I got home from the hospital in the early morning hours after Hady died, I could not go back to sleep. I had trouble sleeping for many nights after that, as the image and memory of my good friend lingered with me.

To this day, I think back with sadness and love, for a great husband and father, a great wrestler and a great friend, taken too soon. ◆

Pro wrestler Jim Hady dies after match

Gentleman Jim Hady, veteran professional wrestler, died at 11:48 last night a short time after participating in a tag-team match at Schofield Barracks. Cause of death has not been determined.

Hady complained of stomach trouble in his dressing room after the match. He showered, dressed and drove to his home in the Pearl City area where he collapsed. His wife, Gail, called an ambulance and he was taken to Leeward Hospital where he was pronounced dead on arrival.

Hady, in his late 30's, was teamed with Lord Blears and Tex McKenzie in one of the feature matches against Ripper Collins, Luke Graham and Frank Allman. The match ended in a draw.

Hady has been wrestling here for the last 18 months. An autopsy was to be held today.

In addition to his wife, Hady is survived by a daughter, Jamie, 5.

The body will be returned to Detroit tomorrow for funeral services.

101

Johnny Barend was a master of unpredictability in locker-room interviews. Opposite: Ed interviews boxing legend Rocky Marciano, who was hired by 50th State Big Time Wrestling as a guest referee at matches staged around the Islands.

CHAPTER 12

In the Locker Room

As the cards for our matches played out every week, I learned that the fans came for the action and the unpredictability. I spied on the crowd in the arena while my big wrestlers were in the ring, smashing into each other or diving off the top ropes. So I heard the gasps, I saw the wide eyes, and I felt the excitement when a match took a turn in any direction.

But I had no idea, when we started doing our TV locker-room interviews, that they would end up going much like our matches did.

Initially, the plan for the interviews was very simple: to promote the matches themselves. We'd get the guys in the studio on camera, they'd talk to me and Lord Blears about who they were up against that week, and it would serve as solid promotion to sell tickets for the live events.

That was the idea. But in what seemed like very little time and through no brilliant plan of ours, the locker-room interviews took on a crazy, unpredictable life of their own.

Boy, did they.

Maybe it was the magic of the camera, close up on the insane faces of guys like The Missing Link, Neff or Johnny Barend. Maybe it had something to do with Lord Blears and me being there as a kind of steadying influence, "keeping it real."

For whatever the reason, those TV interviews, first on Channel 4 at KHVH, then for so many years on Channel 9 at KGMB, became wildly popular with the fans. It was a great bit of good luck for us. The TV interviews became their own little freight train, charging down the tracks to deliver tremendous entertainment every week. And I for one wasn't about to stand in their way.

It was an uncomfortable process for me, settling into my role as "interviewer" in the locker room. After all, for the couple of decades prior to my being that guy holding the microphone, all my focus and energy was in being the best athlete I could be. Using my head and my conversational skills were a far cry indeed from applying a hammerlock or an arm bar.

notes the day before we went on the air, so that I'd know exactly what to say and wouldn't look like a tongue-tied idiot for our Hawaii fans. I'd try to coach the wrestlers in advance about how the interview would go and what we'd talk about.

Then the red light would go on. And I'd panic.

My mouth was like cotton. My mind would race. What was I supposed to say?

It didn't take long for all my advance notes and scribblings to find the trash can. The interviews were going to be ... whatever they wanted to be. They were raw and free-form, and Lord Blears and I got used to just hanging on, going along for the ride.

People have told me in the years since those raging, rambling locker-room interviews that they'd tune in just to see my face. I know it wasn't because I was so pretty. But when Iaukea, or Ripper, or Haggerty got up in my face with their threats and their outlandish claims, I had to be Everyman. To the wrestlers, while the cameras were rolling, I had to wear that expression that either said "I don't believe you" or "Now just settle down" or "You are so full of it!"

As I took my place amid the on-camera combination of the crazy wrestlers' antics, plus Lord Blears' big personality and his engaging British accent, I learned that "less is more" from me. Even in long stretches when I didn't say a word, my face needed to help the fans buy into the anger and bravado the wrestlers put on display.

A couple of words or a stern look from me were all it took. I became like the "Dad" for these big overgrown children around me, just like I was at home with my own kids. I was the dependable guy who kept things in line. And you didn't want to make Dad angry.

When we began doing the TV locker-room interviews, and I was nervous about that red light going on, I thought that just being very prepared would save me. I'd write out questions and plenty of

Somehow, by my seeing these interviews through to the end, with my doubting expressions undercutting the outrageous wrestlers, it said to the TV viewers at home: "Yeah, these guys are crazy. But let's just see what they say next."

And it was critical for me to add credibility, legitimacy and the proper gravitas to the whole crazy proceedings. No matter what, my face needed to say: This is real. Barend really does plan to strangle Iaukea with a tire chain on Wednesday night. This is serious.

In every instance, Job One for Gentleman Ed during the TV interviews was: Try, at all costs, to keep a straight face.

There were many times when the shenanigans of the wrestlers were so outlandish that you could easily hear the entire camera crew laughing in the background. Sometimes the primary cameraman would begin laughing so hard that the fans watching at home would actually see the camera bouncing up and down from his shaking body.

The skeptics would look on those interviews and think it was all just show, a big performance. But there were times in that locker room when I wasn't acting at all, because many of the wrestlers did things that caught me completely by surprise and genuinely amazed me.

Case in point: Mad Dog Mayne.

Mad Dog would take a water glass, then break it apart, put it in his mouth and chew it up piece by piece. I can still hear the sound it made, as Mad Dog's teeth ground up the glass into tiny bits he could swallow. I'd study his jaw, waiting for blood to trickle out onto his chin, but it never did. I have no idea how Mad Dog did it, but he did, right before my wondering eyes.

My work as the straight-faced interviewer in the locker room was always made tougher by the antics of the wrestlers just off camera, pulling stunts and practical jokes that the TV audience never saw, and almost invariably at my expense.

I tried my best to lay down the law. "Listen, guys," I'd tell them, "I don't want any of that screwing around while we're on camera. We have a show to do. So knock it off!"

"Oh, yes, Mr. Francis," they'd all say, acting contrite. "We understand."

Yeah, not really.

On one occasion, I saw the red light go on—my cue that we were live and on the air. I began talking ... but I'd forgotten my microphone.

I kept yammering on, about the upcoming match and the opponents' strategies, but the cameraman knew right away that something was wrong. He stepped from behind his camera and started gesturing at me, to make me understand that my mike was off.

But since I was in the moment, focused on the interview, I just kept talking. I'm certain what I was saying was absolutely brilliant—but no one at home in Hawaii heard a word.

And my "professional" wrestlers, just off camera? They were howling. They figured out what the problem was, and all of them in the studio were laughing their heads off at me, making fun and mocking me.

The wrestlers laughed and hooted so much that it got the camera crew laughing, too, but I still wasn't getting the joke. I just got madder and madder as I tried in vain to continue the interview that no one was hearing.

This went on for a few minutes until one of the TV crew came around behind me and handed me my mike. Then I understood.

What could I do? It was live TV. I tried to act as professionally as I could, taking the mike and starting up as if it had never happened. "Hello, ladies and gentlemen, Ed Francis here," I said, fairly shouting over the continuing laughter of the wrestlers gathered off camera around me. "Welcome to our locker-room interviews ..."

Note to self: Make sure you have the mike when the red light goes on.

I always worked to help the wrestlers make the most out of their moments on camera in the locker-room interviews. I'd play back tapes of their voices to them, so they could hear what they sounded like to their fans. And I'd make other suggestions as well. I told Curtis "The Bull" Iaukea

that he should sit facing away from the camera, just to make him appear to be uncooperative, to infuriate his fans.

Of course, great showmen like Curtis knew how to make their time on camera count.

To maximize his time in the TV locker room, Curtis brought in Harry Fujiwara, who later came to be known as "Mr. Fuji." In reality Mr. Fuji had never wrestled—in fact, when Curtis brought him in, Harry had been checking in cars at a parking garage. But Curtis took him on as his right-hand man, a kind of personal valet. And Curtis always called him "Fooj."

Curtis knew how the fans loved many of the Asian martial arts like karate, and Harry knew some of the moves. So Curtis brought Fuji in to the studio with him, along with some wooden boards. And in that big voice of his, Curtis growled, "Do your thing, Fooj!"

Fuji posed and gesticulated in front of the boards like a great Asian martial artist. Then with a mighty "Hyyyaah!" Fuji shattered the boards to great effect on camera for the live TV audience.

But Curtis knew that he couldn't have Fuji do the same thing week after week. So the following week, Curtis set up to do the same thing, but with a twist ... literally.

Curtis again brought Fuji in, and again he brought the boards for Fuji to smash. But what Fuji didn't know was that Curtis had turned the middle board of the three boards against the grain.

Again Curtis growled, "Do your thing, Fooj!" and held up the boards.

Fuji struck his poses as the great karate expert, and again with a fierce "Haaayyah!" he brought his hand down on the boards.

This time … nothing. They didn't budge.

Again Fuji went after them. "Hyyahh! Haaayyahhh! Heeeeyyahhh!" Nothing.

Fuji didn't want to give up. All Hawaii was watching. Boom, boom, boom. Again and again Fuji hit the boards till his knuckles bled. Still the boards would not yield.

A look of supreme puzzlement—mixed with pain—spread across Fuji's face. Curtis, Lord Blears and I were doing everything we could not to burst out laughing.

Finally, after exhausting every effort to break the boards on live TV, Fuji slunk off camera. It was another moment from our wrestling locker room that the fans would talk about for weeks.

There were times when the action in our live locker-room interviews took its toll on our studio set. Around Christmas one year, we had dressed up the locker room with a beautiful Christmas tree to signify the season. But Curtis Iaukea was feuding at that time with Enrique Torres, a strong, handsome wrestler in from California.

Curtis had been bad-mouthing Torres—much as he did to most of his opponents. But in the live locker-room interview Curtis might have gone a little too far, by saying that Torres was ignorant and uneducated. Curtis got in Torres's face on camera and told him—and the rest of Hawaii—that he was certain Torres never even finished the sixth grade in school.

That enraged Torres, whose "finishing move" in the ring was a dramatic, crowd-pleasing airplane spin. He grabbed Curtis in the locker room, hoisted the big 350-pound Hawaiian up over his head and began to spin him.

Around and around the two men went in the small studio space we had for our locker-room interviews. Torres got dizzy and began to collapse under Iaukea's massive size and weight.

Finally Torres couldn't support Curtis any longer. The two men went crashing into the beautiful Christmas tree, bringing it and all its ornaments to the ground, ruining all the hard work that the TV crew had done to celebrate the season. With Curtis and Enrique still struggling with each other on the floor, in a tangle of Christmas lights, pine needles and broken ornaments, Lord Blears and I looked at each other. It seemed like a good time to go to commercial.

The very best locker-room interviews were those in which one

Johnny Barend dons his trademark top hat to promote an upcoming tag team match—Barend and the Magnificent Maurice vs. Curtis Iaukea and Jim Hady. Opposite: A Lord Blears locker-room interview with Ripper Collins, Pedro Morales and Johnny Barend turns ugly when Morales attacks Barend after Handsome Johnny smashes Pedro's gold watch with a hammer.

Ed interviews the Missing Link and Jim Hady.

wrestler found a way to get the better of an opponent intellectually, without resorting to physical violence at all.

All the fans, of course, loved the visceral thrill of seeing these big men flying around the ring in vicious combat. But the locker-room setting was a chance for fans to see another component of these giants, to peek into the wrestlers' psyches and view their twisted brains on display.

And again, it was Curtis Iaukea who found ways to prove himself to be the thinking man's wrestler.

In the several weeks prior to a big main event with The Masked Executioner (behind the mask, a wrestler named Vic Christie), Iaukea suggested to me that The Executioner was crazy.

Crazy as in mentally unstable. Dangerous. Not to be trusted or taken lightly. In need of serious psychological treatment and therapy. Cuckoo for Cocoa Puffs.

To build this to its fullest impact, on live TV in a locker-room interview Curtis said to me, "Mr. Francis, I know the head of the Psychology Department at the University of Hawaii. But The Executioner is just too dangerous to take up to Manoa. Would it be all right if I spoke to the professor and brought some of his psychological evaluation tools here next week, to test this man?"

I of course told him I thought this was an excellent idea.

Now the fans would spend the week waiting for next week's interview, to see what Curtis would bring, how The Executioner would be tested … and most of all, of course, whether he could pass the test.

Next week came along, and Curtis brought to the studio with him a simple wooden board with cutout shapes of a circle, a star, a square and a triangle. This, Curtis claimed, was a key psychological testing tool at UH, an excellent indicator of mental stability. Curtis said one simple test would show definitively whether The Masked Executioner was of sound mind, or was in fact a complete looney bird as Iaukea claimed.

(Coincidentally, it "just so happened" that we had timed the airing of this live interview with a period when The Masked Executioner was headed to the Mainland for a time, to take him out of circulation in Hawaii and give him a break from local fans.)

With all the attendant drama of a serious, scientific psychological evaluation, Curtis placed the wooden board in front of The Masked Executioner, and handed him the separate shapes—circle, star, square and triangle.

KGMB-TV producer-director Phil Arnone had one camera ease in to a close-up of the board and another camera frame tightly on The Executioner's masked face as he was submitted to the evaluation.

"Now," Curtis intoned in that deep growling voice of his, "Let's see what you can do, Executioner.

Try to put the shapes in their proper places, starting … now!"

Hawaii fans watching our live locker-room interview at home saw in the pukas in The Executioner's mask that his eyes were growing large with anxiety. The Executioner studied the board for a period of time, then carefully, slowly, tried to put
the star shape … in the circle hole.

That didn't work.

He tried to put the triangle shape in the square hole.

That didn't work.

He tried to put the circle shape in the triangle hole.

That didn't work.

The Executioner's attempts slowly got more aggressive, more forceful, as his frustration grew. I stood by with my microphone. Curtis stood by, nodding knowingly, seeing just the outcome he had anticipated for weeks. The TV crew around us in the studio tried their best not to burst out laughing at The Executioner.

Within a few short minutes The Executioner was slamming the shapes down on the wood board, trying to somehow crush them into the holes but having no luck. Slam, slam, slam! He beat the board with the shapes. Nothing fit.

At last The Executioner grabbed the board and, along with the shapes, tossed them all high into the air. With that he stormed off the set, ranting and screaming like the madman that he evidently was. (After all, a university test had just proved it!)

The Executioner was not to be seen again in Hawaii for several months, leaving fans to speculate whether he might have in fact been committed to a mental institution, to get the help he so desperately needed.

One of the most unruly and ill-behaved of our "children" in the locker room was Hard-Boiled Haggerty. He was truly a loose cannon. So I tried—largely in vain—to come up with some cues in advance that might help reel Haggerty in when he went off the rails on live TV.

"Listen," I said sternly to him before we went on the air. "These interviews have a time limit. You can't just keep going forever. We have to get to the commercials."

I could tell that Haggerty was barely paying any attention to me.

"Okay, here's what we're going to do," I continued. "When the camera's on us, they can't see our feet. So when it's time to wrap up, I'll step on your foot. Then you'll know."

Haggerty's mind was wandering. "Got it?" I fairly shouted at him.

"Got it, boss. You bet," Haggerty said, but I wasn't convinced.

And sure enough, as we got into the interview with Haggerty, he was like a runaway horse headed out to the woods. I had no idea what he was talking about, or when he would stop.

Finally, when I'd had enough—and was quite sure the people at home had as well—out of the camera's view I stomped on Haggerty's foot, giving him our prearranged sign to wrap.

But wild horse Haggerty just looked at me on camera and said, "Why are you stepping on my foot?"

Now what? Say something, quick! Think!

In my sternest, most fatherly voice, I squared up to Haggerty and shouted, "Because I want you off the air!"

The light went on for Haggerty. "Oh!" he said. And walked off.

End of interview.

Another of Haggerty's live-interview adventures gave our KGMB producer Phil Arnone a little heart failure. It happened to be Mother's Day, which we had acknowledged on air through the interview with Haggerty.

Then when he had at last run out of steam and was wrapping it up, Haggerty remembered the special day, and chose to honor it in his own uniqe way.

"So that's it, Mr. Francis," Haggerty said, staring me down. Then he turned and looked right into the TV camera. He stepped over to it so his big ugly face filled the whole frame.

"And to everyone else, I just wanna say …" Haggerty growled, "Happy Mother's Day … all you mmmmothers!"

Perhaps the master of unpredictability in the live TV locker-room interviews was none other than Handsome Johnny Barend. From week to week, Lord Blears and I never knew what Johnny was going to do—and that's just the way we liked it.

In preparation for a big match one week between Barend and the faux American Indian wrestler Billy White Wolf, we came in to the studio to find an Indian teepee set up. And sitting cross-legged in front of the teepee was Johnny Barend, mocking White Wolf's supposed cultural heritage.

Phil Arnone set the mood by playing some Indian war drum music in the background. Barend snarled at the camera as it moved in on him. "I'm gonna hit him with a rock!" Barend threatened.

Then Johnny held up the newspaper clipping announcing the match between him and White Wolf. He took the clipping and, as the camera moved in for a close-up on his face, very slowly, methodically, began stuffing the clipping into his mouth. He chewed and chewed, showing audiences that he was a meaner savage than White Wolf, ready to eat him up in the ring.

Another of Barend's trademarks was his cigar. Johnny loved his cigars, and he found ways to make certain they played a prominent role in his on-screen persona.

At one of our locker-room interviews at the HIC, Lord Blears and I arrived to find a full-sized coffin in the corner. At first we weren't certain what it was doing there … until we noticed small puffs of smoke emanating from a hole drilled in the side of the coffin. We drew closer, to smell the telltale cigar smoke and to hear Johnny Barend's unmistakable growling voice from inside the coffin.

So we did what was probably the first and only live television interview in TV history … with a cigar. Barend's cigar, poking out of the hole in the coffin, did his talking for him, waggling this way and that as Barend from inside the coffin told us how he was going to send his opponent for the week to an early grave. We never saw Barend's face for that interview, and neither did the wrestling fans watching at home … but we didn't need to. Johnny's cigar said it all.

Every now and then one of our interviews in the locker room involved some elaborate set-up. And right in the center of one of those was the great Ripper Collins.

We had decided that it would be a terrific promotion to give a car away to some lucky wrestling fan. To do it, we worked it out so that Ripper would promise the fans that when he—and he alone—became the number-one most popular wrestler in Hawaii, he'd personally give the car away.

Great idea. Except that everybody hated Ripper. Or, at least, they loved to hate him.

But at the time we were doing the car giveaway, TV telethons had become very much in vogue. Everyone had a telethon for something, where you'd see the big bank of phone operators on camera, taking calls from viewers making pledges.

I decided that maybe wc should "borrow" from that form just a bit, and do our own "Call-in for Ripper."

I got a bunch of our friends to sit in on our studio set, and we put up some long tables and chairs for them all to sit at, lined with phones.

One little catch: None of the phones was hooked up to anything.

Why not?

Number one: I didn't want to pay the phone company for all the wiring and the hooking up that would go into actually making the phones "hot."

Number two: I didn't have any confidence that our fans would actually call in and vote for the hated Ripper Collins.

So there was Ripper on camera, preening and strutting as always, yelling at the viewers to call in to make him number one if they wanted the car giveaway to happen. Behind him, "operators" were taking calls as fast as they could, first this phone then that one, then that one over there.

All props.

Surprise of surprises: Ripper was voted number one in Hawaii, we did the giveaway and some lucky fan got the car.

Sometimes what people don't know won't hurt them. And—don't believe everything you see on TV. ◆

Victor the Bear plants a wet one on his trainer, the wrestler Tuffy Truesdale, in February 1970.

CHAPTER 13

Airfare for a Bear

The constant search for different and exciting new elements to put in our main event every week for Hawaii fans led us to some crazy promotions, from Indian Death Matches and Texas Battle Royals to Hawaiian Tag-Team Championship Matches and Loser-Leaves-Town Matches.

Probably the wildest—and, in many ways, the most challenging—showcase promotion we did in the Islands was bringing in Victor the Bear for a series of matches with our wrestlers.

Victor the Bear wasn't a gimmicky name for a wrestler, like The Masked Executioner or The Missing Link or Hard-Boiled Haggerty. No, Victor was a real, live, 500-pound grizzly, standing some nine feet tall on his hind feet.

I'd wrestled Victor years earlier in Florida, and I remembered the big crowd that we drew. I also remembered some of the challenges involved. You couldn't whisper in a bear's ear and say, "Let's do this. Now you hold me this way, and I'll take you down." It doesn't work that way with a bear.

I recall the moment I stepped into the ring in Florida and looked into the eyes of that gigantic monster. I was thinking, "How am I going to get through this match?" I tried to just focus on the things the bear's trainer, Tuffy Truesdale, told me, and executed those things to keep the match going.

Tuffy had said to me, "This is what the bear can do. He does a bear hug. If you grab him around his head, he'll swing his body and throw you into the ropes. You come off the ropes and he gives you a bear hug. If you get behind him, he'll put his paw up and give you a flying mare, so you do that."

The early moments of the match in Florida were going well for me. I was working through a series of holds and moves with Victor, and the fans were eating it up. But then the big bear got behind me and wrapped his powerful arms around my waist.

His arms were covered with stiff, prickly fur. A bear's coat is made of thick, coarse hair—it's not like a fluffy little dog's. Tuffy had declawed the bear, so at least I didn't have to worry about that. Otherwise, I would have been sliced into little pieces by the enormous, razor-sharp claws.

I was on my hands and knees with Victor, and I called on my early amateur wrestling training, where you do a sit-out to release your opponent's grip. I pushed up quickly and threw my legs out to escape the bear's grasp, but he was so powerful he just took my full body weight and pulled me hard against his giant body.

Now Victor was on top of me, holding me so tight that I couldn't breathe. I thought my lungs were literally going to burst in the ring. The fans were going crazy. They had no idea that I was fighting for what felt like my last possible breath on Earth.

Finally, just when it seemed I wouldn't be able to continue and was on the brink of passing out, Tuffy the trainer managed to get the bear's attention and pass along some new commands. Victor released his death grip on me and the match continued. I don't even remember who officially won the bout that night—me or the bear. But if the contest was for respect of the raw power of a ferocious predator, the bear won the match, paws down.

Victor's trainer, Tuffy, continued to promote him around the country, based out of Missouri. One day, as Lord Blears and I were faced with still another week's main event to fill, I said, "It'd be great to bring that bear to Hawaii." Be careful what you wish for.

BIG TIME WRESTLING HAWAII

JANUARY, 1979

PROMOTER
ED FRANCIS

SANCTIONED BY A.W.A. AND N.W.A.

PRICE $1.00

VOL. 2 NO. 1

"VICTOR THE GREAT"

IN THIS ISSUE

★RIPPER COLLINS

★VICTOR
The Wrestling Bear

★ARMONDO
GUERRERO

★WHIPPER WATSON

★TOR KAMAKA

★STEVE STRONG

★KARL VON STIEGER

★MR. FUJI

★TAMA SAMOA

★Pretty Boy
LARRY SHARPE

★AND OTHERS

We made the deal, and Tuffy agreed to bring Victor to us. But he'd been travelling with the big bear by trailer and truck around the Mainland. You can't just send a plane ticket off, then have a giant bear sitting in economy class snacking on peanuts on his way to his Hawaiian vacation. Some elaborate arrangements had to be made to get Victor safely caged and loaded onto an airliner for the trip to Hawaii.

When Tuffy and Victor arrived at the airport in Honolulu, I'd laid plans to capitalize on the big day. I'd alerted the Honolulu newspapers and TV stations to drop by to document Victor's arrival, and they obliged. Tuffy brought Victor out of the cargo holding area and positioned him on the stairs to the plane, then handed Victor a champagne bottle filled with Coca-Cola.

Victor stood tall on his hind legs and guzzled the bottle for the cheering crowd. The TV cameras and news photographers loved it. I loved it. As the photographers snapped their pictures for the papers, I could almost count that week's soaring ticket sales. I was in true promoter's heaven.

I had forgotten for the moment that we were dealing with a wild animal.

That fact became painfully apparent in an instant, when one of the news photographers got a bit too close to Victor. His camera's flash spooked the big bear, and Victor bolted down the steps of the plane, with Tuffy giving chase. The offending cameraman took off in the other direction in fear of the bear and shinnied up a light pole nearby.

Tuffy ultimately got Victor calmed down and under control. Luckily for me, the next morning's newspaper headlines did not read, "Newspaper Cameraman Mauled by Ed Francis-Invited Bear." The little mishap on arrival at the airport turned out to be the perfect kickoff promotion for Victor the Bear's Hawaiian adventure.

Then came still another hurdle: dealing with Hawaii quarantine officials, who were not too thrilled at the prospect of having a bear

114

brought to their shores. Suffice it to say that it took some backroom politics and negotiations with local officials to get around some of the quarantine rules. As with anything in life, it's always a matter of knowing the right people in the right places.

We took Victor to the Civic Auditorium to put him in place for his big Hawaii wrestling debut. Tuffy brought him inside, and we found a spot for Victor near the back offices. We chained him to a metal pole, put down a big tub of water and some bear food, and we all went home for the evening.

Much too early the next morning I got an urgent call from Velasco, the Civic's live-in janitor, to come quickly. I hurried in to work, and when I got there I found one very shaken mailman sitting in my office. The mailman had come earlier to deliver a package and found no one at the front door of the Civic. So he went to the rear of the auditorium and found the back door ajar.

When he stepped in, he got the shock of his life. Victor the giant bear reared up on his hind legs, towering over the little mailman, who tossed all the mail he was carrying in the air and ran for the exit. Now he sat in my office, still shaking like a leaf. I gave him all the sincere consolation I could muster, but it was tough not to burst out laughing. What other profession requires calming down a postal carrier after a bear scare?

Now the question became: Who would be the lucky wrestler of my stable in Hawaii to first step into the ring with Victor? The night before Victor's Hawaii debut match, I assembled a handful of my top wrestlers—among them Curtis Iaukea, Ripper Collins, Hard-Boiled Haggerty and Luther Lind-say—for a little "meet-and-greet" session with Victor.

Tuffy had Victor out of his cage—he was still chained to that pole in the back of the Civic.

It probably should have been no surprise to me that no one wanted to get into the ring with the giant creature. I'd planned on Ripper and Haggerty to take on the bear in the next night's match, but they wanted no part of it.

The guys all took a long look, sizing Victor up. That alone was a tall order. Literally.

The room was dead silent, except for the sound of Victor's heavy bear-breathing, kind of a low threatening rumble.

Finally Hard-Boiled Haggerty broke the silence. "You're the promoter, Francis," Haggerty said. "You wrestle the damn bear."

Since it was my crazy idea in the first place, I knew I needed to show my guys that it would be okay. I recalled that, in truth, there is really no way to "wrestle" a bear. At 500 pounds, a bear is easily five times stronger than any man. The trick to working with a bear in the ring is essentially to not fight back.

I told the guys, "It's not hard to do. I've already wrestled Victor in Florida." With that, I took off my shirt and stepped into the ring to demonstrate.

I knew that, when you approach the bear, it stands up on its hind legs and faces you. So I stepped up and faced off against this enormous beast, and he stood up to nine feet high on his hind legs. I went into a wrestling stance and took hold of Victor. He was wearing a muzzle over his snout.

Victor's arrival headlined the January 1979 issue of *Big Time Wrestling Hawaii.*

But as I maneuvered around to show my wrestlers how it's done, my thumb managed to slip down inside Victor's muzzle, where it got lodged inside his cheek. Victor quickly bit down on my thumb, and his vicelike jaws and teeth went through my thumbnail like it was butter. Victor's tooth gouged into the flesh of my thumb and the blood started squirting out and flowing instantly.

I wrapped my fingers over my thumb to hide the damage from the wrestlers who were watching. But there was too much blood to hide. As I stepped away from Victor, a telltale trail of blood from my thumb followed me around the ring.

AIRFARE FOR A BEAR

Hard-Boiled Haggerty said what all the wrestlers were thinking. He looked at the blood gushing from my thumb and said to me, "You're the promoter. You're the expert. You wrestle the damn bear!"

Curtis Iaukea later gave me credit for having a giant-sized portion of courage—even if I was completely crazy to step into the ring with Victor.

Now I had a new fear in my life—the threat of rabies. I was taken to the emergency room, and I couldn't tell the truth to the doctor about what had happened, for fear of them taking Victor away from us. Remember, it was all I could do to negotiate with those quarantine officials to get Victor into the state in the first place.

Victor the Bear wrestles in a match on the mainland. Opposite: Ripper Collins was originally scheduled to wrestle Victor at the Blaisdell Center Arena, but Collins wanted no part of the match-up.

So I told them I'd stepped out behind the Civic to pet a dog there, and the dog had bitten me. But that triggered a call to the cops, who showed up to question me about the dog. I told the cops the dog must've run off and managed to get my thumb stitched up, but the threat of being diagnosed with rabies stayed with me for weeks. Still, I figured that the show must go on. Even if I died, the bear would be in there wrestling Haggerty or somebody, giving the fans a good show.

Eventually, the wrestlers got more comfortable handling Victor in the ring, and we got some good individual matches in our main events over the next few weeks. How to switch it up? We decided to have a Battle Royal with Victor and a whole group of wrestlers in the ring.

That hadn't been done before, so Lord Blears and I sat down with Tuffy to figure out the logistics. We decided to do it cage-match style, putting 10 wrestlers in with Victor and chicken wire around all the ring posts so no one could escape.

We had a huge, sellout, turn-away crowd for the Battle Royal with a Bear at the Civic. I was watching from the stands, in eager anticipation with the rest of the Hawaii fans, as the opening bell rang.

But I could see in those first moments of the match that none of the wrestlers trapped in the ring wanted to take on Victor. They all engaged each other, putting as much space as they could in that small, cramped ring between themselves and the giant bear. As always, I started to sweat. Was this whole hyped match a bad idea?

I breathed a sigh of relief when Luther Lindsay, a true shooter and one of my most skilled wrestlers, made his move to take on Victor. Luther told me later that he could see Victor wasn't getting any action, so he figured he'd better do something.

Now that the 500-pound grizzly was pulled into the fray, the match became a big tangle of flying bodies and falls, all around Victor. But all the flurry of activity must have become too much for the bear. Victor decided he'd had enough of our Battle Royal. He jumped over the top ropes and over the chicken wire we'd erected. No problem at all for him.

Instantly there was pandemonium in the Civic, with fans leaping from their seats out of fear of a bear on the loose. Just down the aisle from the ring I saw a young disabled boy sitting and watching the matches from his wheelchair. Victor leaped directly over the crippled child on his way to the back of the Civic, missing the young boy by inches. I can only imagine what would have happened if Victor had landed with all his weight on the boy, likely crushing him. I suspect it would have also crushed the future of 50th State Big Time Wrestling.

Victor took refuge in a dark, quiet corner of the auditorium, where Tuffy tried to get a chain on him. We all heard Victor's growls and howls echoing through the Civic. It sounded eerily like Victor was saying, "Ohhh, nooo, ohhh, nooo!"

No one was injured, luckily. But I still had a sellout house on my hands, waiting for a show. There was nothing to do but basically start over. Tuffy brought Victor back to the ring. The fans returned to their seats—some in the front rows rather reluctantly. We got the chicken wire back up and the match restarted.

The next day, everyone who'd seen it all happen could tell their friends they were there, the night Victor the Bear got loose inside the Civic. Who wouldn't be proud of that? ✦

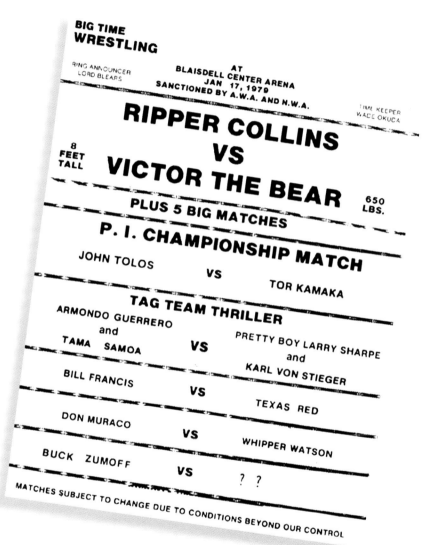

BIG TIME WRESTLING

RING ANNOUNCER
LORD BLEARS

AT
BLAISDELL CENTER ARENA
JAN 17, 1979
SANCTIONED BY A.W.A. AND N.W.A.

TIME KEEPER
WADE OKUDA

8 FEET TALL

RIPPER COLLINS VS VICTOR THE BEAR 650 LBS.

PLUS 5 BIG MATCHES

P. I. CHAMPIONSHIP MATCH

JOHN TOLOS   VS   TOR KAMAKA

TAG TEAM THRILLER

ARMONDO GUERRERO
and
TAMA SAMOA   VS   PRETTY BOY LARRY SHARPE
and
KARL VON STIEGER

BILL FRANCIS   VS   TEXAS RED

DON MURACO   VS   WHIPPER WATSON

BUCK ZUMOFF   VS   ? ?

MATCHES SUBJECT TO CHANGE DUE TO CONDITIONS BEYOND OUR CONTROL

CHAPTER 14

Tokyo Calling

One of the great ways Lord Blears and I got many stars to wrestle for us in Hawaii was to give them a place to work as they were going to or coming from Japan. As the gateway from the U.S. mainland to the Far East, Honolulu was the perfect stopover for wrestlers interested in booking more dates and making the most of their travel.

The man in control of the wrestling operation in all of Japan was a powerful figure named Rikidozan. Riki was a guy with an amazing story. He was actually Korean, born in Japanese-controlled Korea, but early on he took a Japanese name, Mitsuhiro Momota, to avoid being on the receiving end of the discrimination the Japanese practiced against Koreans.

He came by the name Rikidozan when he competed as a sumo wrestler. But, after a short sumo career, he turned to professional wrestling. This was in the years shortly after World War II, when Japan was still stinging from its defeat, and the Japanese needed a hero.

Rikidozan would be that man.

He built his wrestling career by beating foreigners in the ring, most of them Americans, giving his Japanese fans the pride and self-esteem that had been taken from them because of the war. I got to know Riki well, and had tremendous respect for what he had accomplished. Riki became an idol

in Japan. He put pro wrestling on its map … and he became tremendously wealthy.

Riki continued to build his wrestling empire in Japan by turning to promotion. His right-hand man was a guy named Cappy Harada, a former baseball scout with the San Francisco Giants. They took pro wrestling to levels of success that had never been seen before in Japan.

All the while, because of their success and wealth, Riki and his operation became a target for Japanese underworld types like the yakuza, the Japanese mafia. Wrestlers I'd sent over to wrestle for Riki would come back with wild tales of backroom deals and strong-arm men on all the edges of the wrestling scene in Japan.

The stories I heard from Japan reminded me of the old gangster scene in which I grew up in Chicago: Wherever there was money and fame, corruption and violence were lurking, just off in the shadows, but close at hand.

All that history from Japan gave me reason to be uneasy when I got a frantic phone call from Cappy Harada in December of 1963. In clipped, breathless phrases, Cappy told me that Riki had been stabbed in a Japanese nightclub by a member of the yakuza, and that, though they rushed him to the hospital, Riki died on the operating table.

Cappy asked me to come to Japan immediately. He was certain the yakuza had designs to

119

take over Riki's wrestling business. He wanted my help to make sure that didn't happen.

I can't say I didn't have my fears. But I wasn't about to say no. First and foremost, Riki had been a good friend. And friends help friends. But, selfishly, I'd be looking out for my own business interests at the same time. The arrangement I had with Riki to trade and share wrestlers worked well for both of us. That would disappear if Japanese gangsters took over.

I tossed some clothes into a bag and grabbed the first flight to Tokyo I could get. I had no idea what I was getting myself into.

When I arrived in Tokyo, Cappy took me first to visit Riki's widow and their young son. In the main room of their apartment was a shrine to Riki, with his ashes in a small urn and his championship wrestling belt surrounding it. Cappy led me to kneel at the shrine, ring the bell three times and bow my head in respect. I shared a moment with Riki's widow in memory of her husband and my friend.

I checked into my hotel, the Dai Ichi, but my night's sleep was interrupted too early the next morning by a pounding on my door. It was a horde of reporters from the local papers and wrestling magazines, all looking to interview me about my visit and Riki's empire. The language barrier was enormous, but we got through it with lots of hand gestures and broken English. The same language challenges continued that day in a big meeting Cappy had set up for me, with the handful of nervous bankers who had investment money in Riki's various real estate and building projects. With Cappy interpreting, I learned that they all wanted assurances that Riki's empire was safe. I had no idea why they wanted them from me, but I tried my best, through Cappy, to calm them down.

Then, a bombshell: When Cappy dropped me off at my hotel, he told me that members of the yakuza had already moved in on Riki's business office, and he didn't know what to do.

I thought for a moment, then said, "Pick me up first thing in the morning. Bring a van." I had an idea.

When Cappy showed up the next morning with the van as requested, I asked him to take us to the wrestlers' training gym. I knew most of these guys, so when we got there I hand-picked a few and told them what was going on with Riki's empire.

We all hopped into the van, drove over to Riki's business office and made an unscheduled "social call" on the new occupants.

The wrestlers burst through the office doors, shouting and slamming things around. They grabbed the startled yakuza guys and roughed them up just enough. One guy they tossed down the stairs. The message was very clear. The yakuza heard it and left the offices.

So we won the first battle. But it wasn't long before it was made clear to me that the war wasn't over. That night in my hotel room the phone rang. I answered it, and a voice in broken English said, "Get out of Japan if you want to live." I called Cappy, and he posted a guard outside my door.

The next day, Cappy and another of Riki's top lieutenants, a man called Iwata-san, showed me firsthand what was at stake. They took me on a tour of some of Riki's projects in the works: a grand golf-course development and his upscale building projects in Tokyo's high-end Ginza shopping district. It was easy to see why the mobsters wanted to muscle in.

I helped in any way I could during that short trip to secure Riki's business interests for his wrestling empire, his widow and his son. And I must admit that, when my plane cleared the runway on takeoff from Tokyo, headed home to Hawaii, I felt lucky to be alive.

Back in Hawaii, I thought I was clear of the unpleasantness in Tokyo. But just a month later, I got an odd dinner invitation from my next-door neighbors. It seemed odd because we weren't particularly close. And mystery hovered around the neighbor couple. It was known by just a few that both the husband and wife worked for the CIA.

But I accepted, and my wife and I showed up at their door on the appointed evening.

When we stepped into our neighbors' living room, my heart moved up into my throat. Sitting there to greet us was none other than Iwata-san, the top lieutenant of Rikidozan whom I had met in Tokyo.

What the hell was he doing here?

But Iwata-san bowed and greeted me and my wife warmly. We all had a nice dinner together, and in the conversation after dinner I learned that our neighbors had met Iwata years earlier, when they worked in Army intelligence after the war.

Toward the end of the evening, Iwata wasn't feeling well. He was running a fever. So my wife and I offered him a room at our house where he could rest and get healthy. In the couple of days Iwata stayed with us, he told me more about his relationship with my neighbors, and what happened after my trip to Japan.

Iwata-san told me he had gotten to know my neighbors when they helped to free him after they'd caught him dealing in the black market in postwar Japan. About Rikidozan's death, Iwata told me they'd found the guy who killed Riki. They caught him leaving a nightclub and dragged him into an alley. Then they stabbed him multiple times and left him for dead. But somehow, the guy survived, and they were hunting for him again.

Ultimately, Cappy and Iwata and the rest of Rikidozan's team managed to reorganize Riki's business and keep it safe from harm. They even installed an old wrestler friend of ours, Giant Baba, as the new reigning champion and figurehead for the organization.

But on one of my later trips to Japan I learned an interesting footnote from Cappy and Iwata regarding Rikidozan's death. They told me an investigation had revealed that it wasn't the yakuza that had killed Riki. Cappy said Riki had actually pushed someone down in a nightclub men's room, and the guy pulled a knife on him.

Ever the tough guy, Riki was at first slow to go to the hospital, then would not heed his doctors' instructions after his surgery. As Riki lay in the recovery room on an IV drip, the doctors told him not to eat or drink anything else. But Riki ignored them, and sent one of his men to get him a bottle of Japanese cider.

He drank the whole bottle, after which his stomach began to swell. The doctors rushed him back into surgery, but couldn't save him. His own ego was his undoing.

Another version: Years later, I heard that Riki was actually released from the hospital and died a week later of peritonitis, after not receiving proper treatment for the wound.

Corruption and violence were certainly all around Rikidozan, but the true story may have been that he was done in by two equally lethal foes: vanity and arrogance. ◆

CHAPTER 15

Loyal Beyond Belief

The biggest satisfaction I got through our years of wrestling in Hawaii—beyond seeing every seat in the house filled—was the wonderful feedback and friendship from all the wrestling fans we'd meet.

The fans truly came in all shapes and sizes.

One day, Lord Blears and I had just finished lunch at George's Inn, next to the Civic on King Street, when a man came up to us as we were leaving.

The man met us at the door. He was Hawaiian. "Mr. Francis. Lord Blears. An honor," the man said, with a little bow. "I just wanted to tell you. I have enjoyed wrestling so much, for so many years."

We could see that he was welling up with emotion.

The man went on. "I spent many years at Kalaupapa. And following your wrestling meant a great deal to me. So I just wanted to say thank you."

With that, the man held out his right hand to shake ours. His hand had just part of his thumb and one finger.

We shook his hand, thanked him as well for the kind words. We wished him luck.

As he left us, both Lord Blears and I had chicken skin. We were struck by a poignant reality: It was the sobering fact that our crazy, silly, over-the-top brand of entertainment could even make a difference in the lives of the residents of the leprosy colony on Molokai.

been working on, whether I wanted to hear them or not.

For a stretch of several weeks, this fan of ours was working all around Oahu on locations for one of the movies Elvis Presley shot in Hawaii.

Elvis was, of course, a big fan of the Islands. He came over to shoot three movies in Hawaii—*Blue Hawaii*; *Girls, Girls, Girls* and *Paradise Hawaiian Style*—and he broadcast his concert performance, "Elvis, Aloha from Hawaii," around the globe from Hawaii in 1973.

So our little wrestling fan would work with Elvis on his movie during the day, but he'd still show up faithfully at the Civic to see our wrestlers in action every week.

He made sure to give me the latest news from the movie set. I'm sure he thought I'd be interested to know that Elvis practiced karate in his down time on the set, and fashioned himself to be quite the martial artist. "He's a nice enough guy," our fan would tell me, "but he's really into himself."

Of course he was. He was Elvis! Everyone else loved him. Why shouldn't he, too?

A very dear handful of our closest wrestling fans grew to be good, close friends of the Francis family. One in this select group was a wonderful man named Sammy Woo.

Sammy became a calabash uncle to my kids. He loved being part of our extended wrestling family, and he went out of his way to do nice things for us.

One night, when I came home late after the wrestling matches, it wasn't too surprising to find Sammy at our door. I guess he'd followed me home from the matches.

"Mr. Francis," Sammy said at our door with a big, wide grin, "look what I brought you!"

Sammy was holding a great big canvas bag, but it was moving all around as he held it, like it had a life of its own.

He carefully drew open the top of the bag and let me peer inside. In it were dozens of live

Watching some of the characters in the crowd could be almost as entertaining as watching the wrestlers. Opposite: In 1979 at the HIC Arena, Don Muraco (inset bottom) maneuvers Tor Kamata over the ropes, out of the ring and down onto the floor—on the wrong end of a ringside chair. (Appearances to the contrary, Kamata still won the match.)

One of our biggest fans was a little guy who worked in the movie business in Hawaii. He'd come to our matches every week, and he'd come to the back door of the Civic to track me down. As soon as he found me, he'd tell me stories about what he'd

crabs he'd caught for us to eat. They were climbing all over each other.

"Jus' boil 'em up, Mr. Francis. Very tasty!" Sammy said. I thanked him and Sammy was on his way.

The house was dark, and my wife and all the kids were asleep. The only ones awake in the house were the cockroaches.

We had plenty of those, scurrying around whcncvcr you turned the lights on, like in every house in Hawaii. But on this night they gave me an idea.

I took the bag of crabs and dumped them all into the big, deep kitchen sink we had. I left the lights off. Then I went into the kids' bedroom and shook my son Bill awake.

"Bill, you gotta wake up!" I said. "Something terrible has happened!"

I got Bill up, and walked him into the kitchen. He stood there, groggy, trying to focus his eyes in the dark.

"Something terrible has happened to the cockroaches. In the sink. Go look, look close," I said to Bill.

He crossed to the sink and peered down into it in the darkness, his nose almost touching the edge.

I flipped on the light.

There, barely inches from his face, were dozens of the scariest, most gigantic "cockroaches" he'd ever seen.

"Wwwaaaahhh!" he screamed, and bolted out into the yard, running for his life.

The next day, the crabs tasted great to me. For some reason, Bill said he didn't want any.

The fans who came

125

to our matches and followed our wrestlers' exploits were mostly men. But it was hard not to notice from week to week that our matches drew their share of wahines, too.

Sometimes they'd come with husbands or boyfriends. But sometimes they'd come on their own, groups of young ladies who really wanted to see our guys wrestle.

Undeniably, some of these young women made it clear that they hoped to be more to the wrestlers than just casual spectators. These girls—many just 18, 19, 20 years old—would line the aisles as the wrestlers came in or out for their appearances.

They'd gather 'round at the back door before and after the matches. They wanted to meet the guys. They wanted to get autographs. And more than a few wanted to share a well-placed phone number.

Many of these young ladies were stunning. They were gorgeous, Polynesian-hapa mixes of Hawaiian and Chinese, Portuguese haole, or poi bowls of everything mixed together. They were hula dancers, waitresses, mail carriers. They were from all parts of the Islands. But they all had one thing in common: They liked to see big, strong, musclebound men who wore very few clothes in their chosen profession.

Some of the wrestlers were quite happy to make new "friends" whenever the opportunity arose. Curtis "The Bull" and Mr. Fuji would sweet-talk the young ladies. They'd say, "Hey, let's all get together for drinks later." It wasn't uncommon at all to see Curtis or Fuji with a beautiful entourage trailing along with them.

What's the Hawaiian word for "groupie"?

One of Fuji's fans-turned-girlfriends got a little unexpected brush with fame one night out on the town. I'd become good friends with Don Ho and, on many occasions, the wrestlers would go down to see Don's show.

On one of these evenings, Fuji took his latest special girl down to wine and dine her, and enjoy the show together. The evening was going well enough until Don—as he did every night—invited one lucky lady to join him up on stage. That lady on this night happened to be Fuji's girlfriend.

As part of Don's act, just as it happened every night, Don sang to her, he caressed her and he no doubt put his hands where they really didn't belong. That was Don. That was his show.

But that was it for Fuji. He tore backstage after the show, and whatever he said to Don prompted a phone call from Don to me.

"Eh, Mr. Francis," I heard on the line, and I knew immediately that low, lazy, bedroom voice could only be Don's. "Mr. Francis, you gotta call this guy Fuji off. He said he was gonna murder me. He's crazy, this guy. You can't let him kill me."

I dutifully called Fuji into my office.

"Don called," I told him. "You gotta let this thing go."

"Why? Wha'd he say?" Fuji asked. He seemed surprised.

"He said you threatened to kill him."

"I did? Wow. Sorry, boss," Fuji said. "I already forgot about it!"

I guess sometimes those threats from wrestlers seemed more real than they were.

Some of our most loyal fans made themselves known from the unlikeliest of places—like behind prison walls. I discovered this one day when a wrestling fan came to my office at the Civic. He said he had been an amateur wrestler and wrestling coach when he was young, and now he was working at Oahu Prison. He devoted some of his time there to teaching physical fitness and wrestling to the inmates.

The guy told me that all the inmates watched our TV show, and it would mean the world to them to get the chance to meet some of our wrestlers. He invited me to the prison the following Sunday to teach the cons some wrestling moves. I could tell that he genuinely cared about the guys behind bars, and wanted to give them something meaningful in their lives. So I agreed to come by.

On that Sunday, I went in with him to the prison yard to meet the inmates. They had a wrestling ring set up, and we worked on some basic stuff, various holds and moves. They all seemed like good guys. At least that's what I thought.

Over the next month, I worked with them every Sunday, and I felt like the relationship with the guys and our program for them was a great success.

But then things took an unfortunate turn.

One day during that period, I was sitting at my office at the Civic when the morning mail arrived, and in it was a letter from one of the inmates. He wanted to tell me that one of the guys was bad-mouthing me. His letter said that I should report the guy to the warden. I wasn't sure what the guy's motives were in writing me the letter, but I quickly put it out of my mind.

When I went in to Oahu Prison the next week, I was watching two guys working out in the ring when the guy who wrote me the letter sidled up to me.

"Mr. Francis," the guy said in a whisper, "look."

I glanced down to see the inmate pulling something out of his pocket to show me. It was a popsicle stick with a razor blade taped to the end.

"You know that guy I wrote you about?" the con said. "I'm going to take care of him for you. This will shut his mouth."

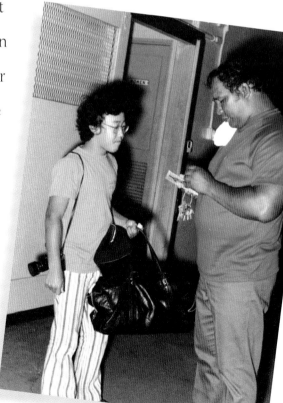

LOYAL BEYOND BELIEF

Well. This was a new one for me. What to do?

"Hey, let me see that," I said to him. He handed over the makeshift weapon.

"You know what?" I said. "There's got to be a better way. I'll take care of it."

I took the guy's blade-on-a-stick and quickly tossed it under the ring, into the dirt. Our eyes met and he got my message. He walked away and didn't bring it up to me again.

I don't know how—or if—those two resolved their differences. But I'd like to hope that I helped my letter-writing friend avoid solitary ... or worse.

Sometimes our fans even got involved in the matches as they were in progress. We had a huge following among the Samoan, Hawaiian and Filipino audiences. Many of the fans were also big boxing fans, and what we put in the ring for them each week was another form of combat for them to enjoy. I was always pleased to see that the Filipino newspapers often carried huge write-ups about our matches.

The crowd in the arena was generally more men than women—many dads would bring their kids to see the action. But as I mentioned, we did have our share of ladies who loved to get up close to the wrestlers. It never failed to surprise me to see even older ladies up in the front row, swinging their purses at the big wrestlers if they happened to spill out of the ring toward the seats.

Often the fans were only too happy to lend a hand.

This was clearly in evidence during one match of mine, a tag-team match with my son Bill as my partner. We were wrestling against the inimitable duo, Ripper Collins and Beauregarde.

I had a headlock on Ripper at one point in the match when he threw me into the ropes. I came off straight at him. We slammed into each other and both went down hard.

Dazed, we both lay on the mat for an instant. Then Ripper started to crawl toward his corner, to tag Beauregarde to take over.

I crawled after Ripper.

Just as Ripper reached up to make the tag with Beauregarde, I reached up behind him. My fingers locked on the waistband of his tights, and I yanked down hard.

What happened next was hardly suitable for family viewing. Ripper's tights snapped down around his knees, leaving his big, bare butt in full view for the crowd to see. They laughed and howled and pointed, screaming at the top of their lungs. It was truly a full moon in Honolulu that evening.

Ripper managed to tug up his trunks and the match continued. Moments later, I tossed Ripper out through the ropes and onto the auditorium floor. I jumped out behind him. Ripper was on his hands and knees, struggling to get up. The fans in their seats were now less than five feet away from us.

I picked one big Samoan guy out of the crowd and shouted to him, "Give me your belt!" The guy was confused at first. "Your belt, your belt!" I shouted. The guy got the message and handed me his belt—quite a weapon, given the guy's girth—and I began whipping Ripper with it.

As I lashed Ripper's back right next to the crowd, the fans could see the welts rise immediately. Giant red marks covered Ripper's big haole back, much to the delight of the crowd.

Ripper tried to escape, running with that big, fat body of his in the direction of the locker room. Of course, it was easy for me to keep up with him, and I chased Ripper through the arena, whipping him like a jockey uses his crop at the finish of the

Kentucky Derby. The referee counted us out and disqualified both tag teams, but I didn't care. Not when the crowd was cheering like that.

There were also all sorts of social occasions when we met our fans. It happened with regularity at the home of our jack-of-all-trades Nolan Rodrigues. He was our "go-to guy" who built our wrestling ring for the TV studio, refereed many of our biggest matches and had friends who could get anything done for us overnight. He also became a very close friend of the Francis family.

I can't count the number of Rodrigues family events and celebrations that we enjoyed through our many years together. One such event was an amazing luau spread in Waimanalo, with marvelous local food, dozens of good friends ... and free-flowing Primo beer.

As the party wore on into the evening, one of Nolan's guests, a big Hawaiian fellow, had clearly been overserved. I noticed him sort of weaving among the partygoers. His eyes weren't focusing too well. He wasn't a young man, maybe in his late 50s.

Somehow, through his inebriated haze, he managed to spot me sitting in a chair near him.

"Eh, Meestah Francis," he slurred. "Now you wrestle me!"

The guy raised his arms in a drunken wrestling stance, and beckoned me. He swayed precariously. It looked like the alcohol alone was going to wrestle him to the ground.

"No, no," I protested, holding up my hands. "I don't want you to hurt me."

"No, you come!" the guy insisted. He moved a little closer to me.

The crowd around us started paying attention to our little exchange. Our host, Nolan, was looking at me with a smile. I could tell he was hoping I'd stand and make a match of it.

I certainly didn't want to disappoint our host. So I stood.

The guy rushed at me, stumbling forward.

As soon as he got to me, I grabbed his arm and put an arm-drag on him, pulling his wrist and swinging him around in one quick move so that I was behind him.

I took my foot and swept his legs out from under him. He went down like a family-size bag of Hinode rice. I lay over him and dropped my forearm in a cross-face hard against his nose.

"Ow, ow, ow, ow, ow, ow!" he screamed, though I wasn't hurting him at all.

That's when the ref would have counted him out.

Our wrestling "match" probably lasted around 6.2 seconds. Maybe less.

I stood up, then helped the guy to his feet. A friend of his took his arm, and they staggered away.

I had encountered other fans from time to time in my career, both in Hawaii and elsewhere, who could clearly benefit from a little "education" about the wrestling trade. Many fans liked nothing better than to get in our faces and taunt us about our craft.

Such was the case for me at one point when I was wrestling in a match in Canada. I was working with the Canadian Open Heavyweight Champion there and, as we were sitting around after a match, we were approached by a group of fans who wanted to talk.

We talked about different matches and outcomes and wrestling holds that led to those outcomes. I happened to mention the "sleeper hold," and one of the fans in the group started laughing.

"The sleeper hold?!" he said, mocking me. "Wow, that is so phony!"

"You think so?" I said quickly. All his friends got very quiet, along with the guy's wife, who was in the group. I got up out of my chair. "Let's just see how this thing works."

The fan was sitting in a rocking chair across from me, and I walked around behind him and applied the sleeper hold.

In seconds the fan's eyes closed. He began to drift off. He blacked out completely … and proceeded to pee in his pants.

I've been in some awkward moments in my life, but this one definitely ranked right up there. You could've heard a pin drop. No one said a word. His wife and his friends just stared at this soaking-wet wrestling fan, asleep in his rocker.

I rocked him a couple of times, just for good measure, then started massaging his neck to get the blood flowing again.

The sleeper hold is really very simple: You press down on the carotid artery that feeds blood up to the brain. If it's done right, and the brain is deprived of that blood flow for a quick moment, it induces unconsciousness very quickly.

(With my new sleeping friend in the rocker, the urination was just a bonus.)

But a word of caution: My applying the sleeper hold was a dangerous way of proving a point. The technique may be quick and effective, but it can have unwanted consequences.

That also happened to me with another group of fans, coincidentally, again in Canada. The fans, who were guys on a minor league baseball team there, were mouthing off to me about wrestling. And this time their heckling had actually made me angry.

I put the sleeper hold on the most boisterous guy in the group, and I put it on him pretty good. He went out like a light. But after he went out, I had a tough time bringing him to again. It worried me enough that I almost called an ambulance for him. Fortunately, the fan did come around, and he was fine.

Lesson to be learned: Kids, don't try this at home.

Plenty of the wrestling fans in the Islands would seek out me and my wrestlers, and want to show us their stuff. Many seemed to think they were just as tough as us. But I was careful to avoid conflict at all costs, and counseled my wrestlers to do the same.

First, it was just good business sense. The last thing we needed was glaring newspaper headlines or assault records.

Second, it was the safest route to take, especially when any one of us could be outnumbered and overwhelmed.

At a pizza place one night, a group of five or six Samoans came up to me.

"Eh, Messtah Francis! Gentleman Ed!" they were all calling. They challenged me to an arm-wrestling competition.

"No, I'm getting too old for that," I declined, laughing.

But they insisted. They moved in and tightened the circle around me.

I'd been in this situation before. If it was one on one, maybe. But I wasn't about to take on a half-dozen guys. I improvised.

"Hey, did you guys hear what Neff Maiava did in the locker room yesterday?" I asked them.

Their eyes brightened. They wanted to hear. I knew Neff was their god.

I made up some story about Neff that got them laughing. We talked about Neff. Then we talked about Al Lolotai. We talked about the matches the guys had been to, the matches they wanted to see. They started arguing among themselves about who was the weakest of our wrestlers.

Fifteen minutes later, they bought me a beer. My new best friends.

But sometimes …

Sometimes it was hard not to mix it up a little. On one of our wrestling trips to Hilo, I had Tosh Togo, Curtis Iaukea and Gene LeBell with me at a little hotel restaurant.

It had been raining all night, and we took a table to wait out the storm and have a couple of beers. At a table near us were a couple of local guys. They'd been drinking there awhile. Maybe a tad too long.

They started mouthing off to us. But not to all of us. They were picking on Gene LeBell, the redhead haole in our group.

"Eh, dis guy, you a wrestler?" they taunted Gene, then looked to me. "You let him wrestle for you, Meestah Francis? I could take him, any time."

They kept talking trash until I decided it was wisest to vacate the premises. I got all my guys up, we paid our tab and headed out.

There was a flight of stairs leaving the restaurant. As we got to the bottom of the stairs, the local guys emerged behind us from the restaurant.

"Eh, haole, what, you chicken, brah? Gotta hide behind your boys?" one of the guys called after Gene. He started down the steps.

Neither of the guys had any idea that LeBell was a world-class judo champion who had trained for years, and had beaten the very best in Japan. The guy coming down the steps had no clue what was waiting for him at the bottom.

I looked at Gene. "Well?" I said. "What do you think? Let's just not end up with the cops here, okay?"

Gene nodded and smiled.

When the guy got to Gene, LeBell grabbed him and gave him a high hip-lock. He sent the guy flying out into the rainy Hilo night, where he landed with a splash in a mud puddle.

LeBell crossed, did it again and shoved the guy's face into the mud.

Now I crossed over to him and gave him one kick in the side for good measure. I leaned down close to his face and asked very politely, "Want some more?"

He didn't.

As we walked away, my wrestlers all clapped me on the back. "Nice job, Mr. Francis," they teased. "We didn't know you were so tough!"

Never kick a man when he's down. Unless you've got good people behind you. ◆

The wrestlers came in all shapes and sizes. Opposite: Little Brutus and Sky Low Low report for work at the Civic Auditorium.

CHAPTER 16

What Nobody Saw

Many of the strangest things that happened to our day-to-day wrestling operation in Hawaii during our glory days were things that never went before the eyes of the fans.

On the surface, our crowds only knew that there were more matches to see every week and, if they couldn't get to the matches in person, there were the TV shows to watch. But behind the scenes there were always all sorts of ongoing dramas and crises brewing.

Some of the dramas were about money, some were about politics.

Some were about both.

At one point, the State of Hawaii Boxing Commission got it in its heads that, along with boxing, it should be regulating wrestling matches as well. Our matches.

What did this mean? For me, it meant one more giant-sized worry. The Boxing Commission's involvement in our operation could have served as our death warrant.

For starters, it would mean that the Boxing Commission took 10 percent right off the top of our profits. Our margins were slim enough and money was tight enough that this alone could have done us in.

Beyond that, the Boxing Commission was lobbying to legislate our business in a variety of

other ways. Its involvement, if it was approved, would have meant blood tests for our wrestlers, physical exams, licensing, doctors on site for the matches—all the sorts of requirements already in place for boxing matches.

Now, don't get me wrong: The last thing in the world I wanted was for any of our wrestlers to get hurt, on a match night or at any time.

Number one, all our wrestlers were friends of mine. I cared about them.

Number two, they were the meal tickets. If they didn't stay healthy, we had no show.

But what the Boxing Commission wanted to impose on our operation was an overlay of administrative costs and procedures that would have proved devastating to us.

That nagging "worry spot" on my chin, symptom of the stress I was always carrying, was never redder or larger than when I was preparing to face off against the Boxing Commission. It was like Showdown at the Hawaii Wrestling Corral. Only the strong would survive.

Approval of the Boxing Commission's proposal to regulate us fell to the Hawaii State Legislature. The fate of Mid-Pacific Promotions was in its hands.

But I had some friends ...

It took some phone calls. Let's just say some arrangements were made.

Thanks to those friends in the right places, each time the Boxing Commission proposal came up for consideration at the State Capitol, certain politicians found ways to pigeonhole it so that no action was taken.

In the end, no one was the wiser. The fans kept coming to our matches, and they kept watch-ing our TV shows. We made sure ourselves that if, God forbid, any of our wrestlers needed medical care, they got the attention and treatment they deserved.

Mid-Pacific Promotions and 50th State Big Time Wrestling continued, business as usual. The State Boxing Commission kept its paws off. Done deal.

Another thing that most of our fans never saw was what our wrestlers were up to in their time outside the ring or away from our TV locker-room interviews.

I was busy enough with the business side and with my own family that I seldom did too much socially with the wrestlers. The guys I was closest to—guys like Curtis "The Bull" and Jim Hady, Nick

Bockwinkel and a few others—I did see from time to time away from the matches.

Of course, when they had the chance, the guys would go out, often together with other wrestlers. After all, they were in Hawaii! Their mindset was: We're on vacation. Why shouldn't we go looking for a good time when we're not in the ring?

As a result, my challenge was trying to make sure our Hawaii fans didn't see any of our in-the-ring "arch rivals" out chumming around together in public.

Imagine: I'd just spent the past month in TV interviews, newspaper ads and prelim matches setting the stage for the grand winner-take-all, fight-to-the-death rivalry between, let's say, Curtis "The Bull" Iaukea and Andre the Giant.

Many of our main-event matches even had the added cachet of being sanctioned belt matches, to lay claim to the Hawaiian Heavyweight Champion crown and other titles.

How was I to explain it—to the newspapers or to anyone else who might be listening—if Curtis and Andre were spotted down at Don Ho's show having drinks together and acting like BFFs?

As best I could, I tried to lay down the law with the guys: No fraternizing in public. It seemed like such a petty and intrusive way to run a business, by even attempting to direct or control what the guys did on their own time.

Still, it needed doing. One of the great blessings about Hawaii is its small-town feel. Maybe it's not quite that "everyone knows everyone," but everyone knows someone, who knows someone else. And they'll talk.

To keep people from talking—or *Star-Bulletin* and *Advertiser* columnists from writing—about which wrestler they saw out with another wrestler having drinks when they were supposed to be bitter enemies, I "asked nicely" of my wrestlers that they keep their distance in public.

My request wasn't always heeded. We had our share of moments when fans busted supposed

ring rivals in public together. But, for the most part, our wrestlers would make an honest effort to keep their private lives, their private time and their friendships private. Our living depended on it.

One of the notable exceptions to that rule was an episode involving Curtis Iaukea and a huge 6-foot, 9-inch wrestler from Texas named, appropriately enough, Tex McKenzie.

With the jumbo size of both their physical stature and their personalities, Curtis and Tex were two guys who were tough to hide. Low key was not in their repertoire.

135

The night Curtis and Tex took "Broadway" Joe Namath out on the town in Honolulu, they were definitely not flying under anyone's radar. Namath was, of course, the superstar New York Jets quarterback, MVP of Super Bowl III, and he'd come over to the Islands for a big speaking engagement. Curtis knew Joe from his own time playing pro football (Curtis played in the Canadian Football League), so he'd invited Joe to join him "for a few drinks."

As so often happens, a few turned into quite a few more than a few, at a huge party Curtis and Tex threw for Joe at the Ilikai Hotel. The evening's celebration did not escape the attention of the newspapers in Honolulu. They were only too happy to point out that Curtis and Tex most definitely did not look like the mortal enemies they were supposed to be in the ring.

To make matters worse, the late-night partying proved to be a bit too much for Broadway Joe. He slept in the next day and missed the speaking engagement he'd been brought to Hawaii to attend.

In truth, Curtis Iaukea's big personality—accompanied by his extra-large stature and his enormous appetite for life—extended well beyond the ropes of the wrestling ring. To say that Curtis enjoyed having a good time was a world-class understatement.

In fact, when the fun stopped for most people—when the bars closed in Waikiki—it was much too soon for Curtis. That's why he opened his own underground after-hours club there, so the party could continue for him and his friends after other places closed up for the night.

Lady wrestlers, including local girl Lei Lani Kai (left) were always big draws. Opposite: Lady Moolah was a standout athlete who also helped train new women wrestlers.

136

To Curtis, it didn't seem unreasonable at all to have a place where he and his friends could gather, perhaps with his latest collection of "new" friends of the female persuasion, to have a few more cocktails late into the evening.

One small problem: It was against the law.

The Honolulu Liquor Commission laid down the rules about the hours permissible for serving alcohol. But Curtis didn't play by the rules.

That's why I got the call late one night, or early one morning, depending on your perspective. The call roused me out of a deep sleep. I fumbled for the phone. At four in the morning, very few calls come in bringing good news.

"Francis," the voice said. "Curtis." I knew that.

"I'm in jail," Curtis continued. "Cops brought me in. Breaking the liquor curfew laws."

I processed this, still groggy with sleep. It was silent for a moment on both sides of our conversation.

Finally, I said, "Okay. What do you want me to do?"

A pause, then a sheepish question from Curtis. "Get me out?"

Why me? And why at this hour?

"Curtis. Your Dad's the police captain. Why don't you call him?" I said.

This met with some more silence, until I agreed to come down to the station.

By the time I got there, Curtis had called his Dad—a captain with

137

never-ending quest for novel wrestling cards for our Island crowds, we couldn't see any reason they wouldn't be welcome in Hawaii.

We learned very quickly that many folks in Hawaii felt differently about this. It seemed everyone we spoke to had an opinion about lady wrestlers. Most of my friends in Hawaii told me that Christian groups would oppose letting ladies in the ring.

Even Ralph Yempuku, the manager and boxing promoter at the Civic, told me, "Francis, you better not do that. It's wrong to expose women's bodies in the ring like that."

This made me certain I wanted to bring lady wrestlers to Hawaii.

HPD—who also showed up, madder than hell. With a little very reluctant help from Captain Iaukea, the Bull made bail. But his own private-party after-hours club operation became a thing of the past.

Sometimes, new and different elements would show up for the matches our fans saw, and the fans never had any idea how they got there. One of those things was a steady stream of lady wrestlers Lord Blears and I began bringing in from the Mainland.

There was already a fairly well-established circuit of lady wrestlers working across the U.S., many of whom both Blears and I had crossed paths with when we wrestled on the Mainland. A woman we knew named Mildred Burke booked many female wrestlers for venues nationwide. In the

Still, to get one more opinion, I went to visit Thurston Twigg-Smith, publisher of *The Honolulu Advertiser*. Twigg-Smith listened to my plans and mulled them over for a moment. Then he told me the same thing I'd been hearing: that seeing ladies fighting with each other, in skimpy costumes, would likely be viewed as exploitative and inappropriate for audiences in Hawaii.

I walked out of his office with one thing on my mind: I guess I'd better bring the girl wrestlers in.

So in they came by the planeload, and they were a big hit with our fans. Some of the ladies were excellent wrestlers—some were not—and many of them were beautiful girls.

Probably the strongest pure wrestler of the

bunch was a woman who wrestled under the name Lady Moolah. She helped train all the other lady wrestlers and was a real asset to our operation. The ladies became a fixture off and on in Hawaii for years, and they always put on a good show on the prelim card to help boost the main event that night.

When some of the lady wrestlers first got to the Islands, Lord Blears and I decided to have a little fun with them, as a welcoming gesture. I had put the four ladies up at a hotel in Waikiki, then I had Lord Blears call them and tell them that a newspaper reporter was stopping by to interview them.

The ladies had never met me before, so I showed up at their hotel room in a button-down shirt and tie with my hair slicked back, pretending to be the newspaper reporter. I whipped out my reporter's notepad and pen, and started asking them questions.

I began with the kinds of questions the ladies might expect in an interview for the paper: How they got started wrestling, how they trained, what their schedule was like and what they were hoping for on their visit to the Islands.

Then I turned the questioning. I told them that it seemed to me—just an innocent newspaper reporter—that a lot of the fans think wrestling's phony. They kind of laughed and deflected the question, but I pushed on.

"In fact," I pressed them, "a lot of people might say you're all fakes. Just phonies. Just play acting." They weren't laughing now.

I could see it in their faces. Who does this guy think he is? What's his deal?

I wouldn't let up. "Yeah, some people say your matches are fixed, that it's all staged, you don't even ..."

Before I could finish, one of the lady wrestlers came at me, eyes blazing.

"Listen, Mister," she shouted, "who do you think you are, coming in here like that, giving us sh#%?" She started shoving me, hard, with both hands, pushing me back toward the door I'd entered.

"You can just get the hell out of here, Mister, with your ..."

Now it was my turn to interrupt.

"Ladies, ladies, relax," I laughed. "I'm Ed Francis. I booked you here. Welcome to Hawaii!"

There was a quick laugh from the ladies. But then the face of the one who'd been shoving me clouded with anger again. She realized they'd been had by the fake newspaper reporter.

"That's not funny, Francis!" she shouted. "We got all dolled up to be interviewed ... for nothing?!" She went right back to shoving me out the door.

At least all the ladies were certain to remember their first day in Hawaii.

Bringing ladies over to wrestle on our cards at the Civic and the HIC was just one of the many wrinkles Lord Blears and I introduced to the Island fans. Another was bringing over midget wrestlers, both ladies and men. They were, once again, something different, and a new and interesting spectacle for our fans.

Opposite: When Ed and Lord Blears began bringing in midget wrestlers—both men and women—the matches provided a new and interesting spectacle for local fans.

Since Blears and I wore every hat and were all things to all people in our wrestling operation, it fell to us to go pick up the lady midget wrestlers when they arrived in Honolulu. We drove down to the old airport to collect them and waited for them by the baggage-claim area.

We knew it wouldn't be too hard to pick them out in the crowd getting off the plane. Soon enough, the two midget ladies showed up for us wearing their finest clothes—and high heels. It just struck both Lord Blears and me as so odd—and funny—that these ladies, who might have been all of four feet tall, were wearing high heels to make them maybe 4 feet-2 inches tall.

I left Lord Blears with the little ladies, and went to go bring the car around. But I'd give

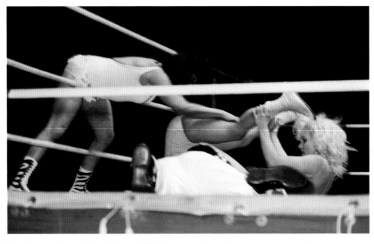

anything today to have a photo of the scene that greeted me when I returned: Here was hulking, lumbering Lord Blears, trudging along loaded down with luggage, flanked on either side by a lady midget with her high heels clicking through the airport baggage area. Clickity, clickity, click click click.

Heads were turning from every direction to watch this spectacle, and Lord Blears' face was beet red. Just one more task to put on the job description for a couple of wrestling promoters: personal valets for lady midgets.

Something else that none of our wrestling fans saw were the various side businesses and enterprises that many of our wrestlers were involved in outside the ring. Occasionally, the guys would consult with me about these businesses. Too often these consultations would involve requests to borrow money from me. And some of the guys' outside businesses were things I really didn't care to know about.

I recall reading the newspapers in Honolulu one day about a big bust and raid on a local clothing store. The articles said the cops busted the store for selling stolen and knock-off label counterfeit merchandise.

I didn't think too much about it, until just a couple of days later, when Harry "Mr. Fuji" Fujiwara showed up in my office.

"Mr. Francis," Fuji said, "you want some shirts? Nice Hawaiian shirts?"

It at first sounded like just one more of Fuji's crazy side businesses. Along with being a great showman in the ring and in our locker-room interviews, Fuji always had all sorts of offbeat diversions going on. For instance, at a big gathering of all our wrestlers once at the Biltmore Hotel, Fuji supplied all the food. He put on an incredible spread of great Chinese, Japanese and Hawaiian food, and we all enjoyed it. No one asked where it came from.

So Fuji's offer of shirts seemed like one more crazy sidelight of his. "You're selling shirts now?" I asked him.

"Not selling, giving," Fuji said with a smile. "It's a gift. For you!"

With that, Fuji stepped out of my office, then returned with his arms loaded down with a couple of dozen beautiful, top-quality Hawaiian shirts. He deposited them on my desk.

"Nice, eh?" Fuji said proudly.

Now I was getting a little suspicious. "Where'd you get them?" I said. I began thinking about the article I'd just read, about the local clothing store raid that went down.

Fuji backed up a step, and I could tell he was having a little trouble with an answer. "Uh, well," Fuji stammered, "from a friend of mine. I can't tell you the whole story."

I thanked Fuji, but told him I had all the shirts I needed. I could see Fuji was a bit crestfallen that his boss wouldn't accept his kind "gift." But he gathered up the pile of shirts and was on his way.

They called it "cockaroaching." My guys made a joke out of it. It wasn't stealing. It was just … cockaroaching.

Our fans also never saw the many ways in which our wrestlers risked life and limb in their spare time. These guys were all risk-takers in a variety of ways, no matter how I tried to advise them otherwise. My son Russ had a hand in one of these adventures.

Russ was an avid skydiver. He had thousands of jumps under his belt. As a licensed pilot, Russ also would take others up to enjoy the sport he loved.

When a couple of my wrestlers asked to go skydiving, Russ was happy to make it happen. Of course, my guys asked Russ. They didn't ask me. If I'd known about it, it would never have happened.

Remember: These wrestlers were all grown men who led their own lives and made their own decisions. I didn't own them. But the day these guys took off with Russ was the day of one of our big matches. Not quite the best day to take a dare and jump out of an airplane.

The wrestlers were skydive beginners, so Russ gave them some training and instruction on the ground, then up they went into the skies over Oahu. Russ pushed them out of the plane, and down they came.

They deployed their chutes as rehearsed on the ground. But Rick Martel, a strong Canadian wrestler who weighed in at around 225, wasn't quite ready for the winds that would take him as he floated down toward Earth.

To bring female wrestling to the Islands, Ed and Tally Ho tapped into a well-established circuit of lady wrestlers working across the country.

The winds pushed Martel well off course and away from his landing target, where he came crashing down into some barbed wire. Martel managed to survive the crash, but it left him with a nasty gash under his arm, taking him out of my main event that night. It was a match that had, of course, been heavily hyped and promoted in advance.

Martel was very lucky that he just escaped with some cuts and scrapes and bruises, and didn't suffer a much worse fate. Lucky for Martel … and even luckier for my son Russ, who would have had to answer to one even angrier father if things had turned out worse. ◆

141

Ed floors a tag team opponent as
Billy Francis looks on. Opposite:
In February 1972 the Francis tag
team defeats Big Daddy Siki and
Mad Dog Mayne.

CHAPTER 17

A Family Affair

As much as I worked, and as devoted as I was to making our wrestling business a success, it was really all toward one simple end: to give my family a comfortable life and lifestyle in Hawaii.

I had no lofty designs on being a giant power in the national wrestling promotion ranks, or personally becoming a millionaire. I just didn't want my wife and kids to ever experience anything like I'd known as a kid in the Depression, when food was scarce, clothes were borrowed and home was the projects.

And as busy as I was at work, I still managed to find time for home and family. Two of my four sons—Russ and Bill—played football and basketball and wrestled in high school, and I found the time as often as I could to get to their games and matches.

My boys were mini-celebrities in their school set, because everyone knew their Dad was on TV and he put on the wrestling matches. But their elevated profile at school made it all the more newsworthy around campus when they got out of line.

When Bill and Russ were both playing football and wrestling at Kailua High School, it was no great secret that some students in their class were drug users—their classmates called them the "dopeheads"—who would hide out just off campus on what they called Marijuana Hill.

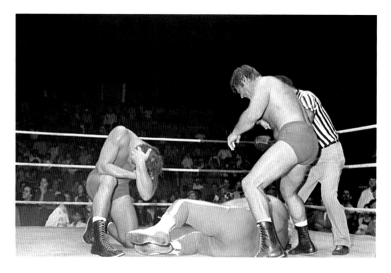

That crowd was always mocking "the jocks" like Bill and Russ, giving them a hard time. So one day my boys decided to take matters into their own hands. They grabbed three or four of the dopeheads and, in order to shut them up and teach them a lesson, locked them in a storage closet on campus.

That was one of the times I got a phone call from the Kailua High School principal.

Another time was when Bill and Russ actually got into it with each other on campus. The wrestling coach at one point pitted Bill against Russ, to wrestle each other when they were training on the team. (I could have told him that was not a good idea.)

That afternoon, Bill and Russ had begun on the wrestling mat in the gym at school. But their "training match" turned into a war between brothers. It spilled off the mat and through the gym, where together Bill and Russ broke a door down during their fight.

Ed, the principal's on the phone for you. Again.

Bill also got a close-up look at the real dangers of wrestling when he went up against a big Samoan opponent for a championship in high school. The Samoan outweighed Bill by a good 60 or 70 pounds. At one point in their match, Bill picked his opponent up, and they came crashing down on the mat together.

But the way they fell twisted Bill's arm and broke it, and the bone in Bill's arm pushed straight out through the skin. From my seat in the gym, my stomach turned.

They of course rushed Bill to the hospital, and I was in the E.R. with him as the doctor realigned the bone before they put a cast on. Bill was in excruciating pain, but he hardly made a sound as the doctor worked. He was one tough kid.

Years later, both my sons' wrestling skills came full circle when I invited them to wrestle for me on pro cards for 50th State Big Time Wrestling. At first it was a difficult transition for Bill. He was a big guy, with real skills—what we'd call a true "shooter"—and it was hard for him not to do his opponents some serious damage. So he'd essentially overcompensate and let men with lesser skills beat him up.

(And many of my wrestlers were only too happy to oblige. Hey, we get to beat up Francis's kid! Cool!)

It took a while for Bill to strike the proper balance as a pro. But soon enough he became one of the guys, holding his own against many of our top performers, and even wrestling in tag-team matches with his old man. It was a good, promotable addition to that week's card: Who wouldn't want to come see Gentleman Ed and his kid teaming up?

Even though Bill was the promoter's son, anyone could see at a glance that, with or without his connection to me, he was perfectly suited to be a pro wrestler. At the time he was 6 feet 5 inches, around 285 pounds. He worked out and lifted weights, so most of those pounds were solid muscle. His arms were 20 inches. When we walked in Waikiki, tourists would stop and stare. And they weren't staring at me.

144

It was only a matter of time before Russ joined the family business for a period of time, both as a solo wrestler and in tag-team partnerships with brother Bill.

By the time Russ came to join us, he'd already played as a tight end for the New England Patriots and the San Francisco 49ers in the National Football League. Russ was selected for three Pro Bowls and four All-NFL teams, and he played a key role in San Francisco's win over Miami in Super Bowl XIX.

One of his matches for us demonstrated just how seriously folks took their pro wrestling. It happened out at Schofield Barracks' Conroy Bowl. Russ was scheduled in a tag-team match on the card, and one of his NFL friends, the great linebacker Jack Lambert of the Pittsburgh Steelers, came to watch the match.

The match took a turn at one point, with Russ's opponents getting the better of him. Down Russ went as the "bad guys" beat on him relentlessly, throwing him out of the ring.

Out in the crowd, Lambert went berserk. He came running from his seat to ringside, grabbing the wrestlers in Russ's defense. Lambert didn't like seeing his NFL friend get beaten. Russ had to take

Jack aside the first chance he got and let him know that he'd be okay.

Away from the wrestling ring, our family at home was not very different than any other busy household full of kids growing up in Hawaii. I had my own share of household chores, doing things like taking out the garbage and doing the dishes. I've always said that, when I die, there are four words that should go on my tombstone: He did the dishes.

Our extended family had gotten bigger in Hawaii after I brought over my wife Arlene's mother, brother and sister to the Islands. I had a next-door neighbor when we lived on Mokapu Boulevard in Kailua who worked with the commissary service for Pan American Airlines, and he helped some of my wife's family find jobs with Pan Am. When we weren't all working, the family enjoyed plenty of beach, surf and play time, and we loved our life in Hawaii.

Father and son enter the ring on Christmas night in 1969, on the occasion of Billy's first professional wrestling match. Opposite: Billy on the wrestling team at Kailua High School.

We were good friends with popular TV personality Napua Stevens, who'd been kind enough to have me on her TV show many times promoting our wrestling matches. It happened that Napua and my wife were pregnant at the same time, and my son Sonny (Ed, Jr.) was born on the same day at Kuakini Hospital as Napua's son.

A year later, we planned a big one-year baby luau with Napua for both our sons at the house on Mokapu Boulevard. The invite list was so big that we decided to take down the fences to our neighbors' yards and put in giant tents. Napua brought in a couple of 600-pound pigs, roasted luau-style up at Kamehameha Schools, and she got the Kam Schools girls to help out in the food prep and serving.

The crowd was so big that parking became a challenge. There was a median strip down the

A FAMILY AFFAIR

middle of Mokapu Boulevard, and folks who couldn't find parking began putting their cars on the strip. This didn't sit too well with the cops, who arrived and began ticketing illegally parked cars until they ran out of tickets. Then they gave up and left us alone to have our party.

All told there were more than 1,000 people in attendance that day—for a couple of one-year-olds!

In the years ahead, as the Francis family continued to grow, I'd take my son Sonny and my young daughter, Pixie, down to Kailua Beach. There was a canal that fed down to the water, and we'd rig up homemade poles and bait to try to catch tilapia. Then we'd hunt down what we could find in the tide pools dotting the shore.

When I'd find a small crab trying its best to hide from us, I'd stick my big thumb down into its crab hole and let it get a grip on me. Then I'd yank my thumb out, screaming in pain for full effect, as Sonny and Pixie looked on, wide-eyed. At least for those few wonderful hours on the beach at Kailua, I wasn't worrying about the next week's wrestling card.

Of course, child care wasn't without its own brand of stress. We'd go to Ala Moana Center virtually every Sunday morning, where the top pastime on my kids' list was letting the koi in the shopping center's ponds suck on their fingers.

But on one ill-fated Ala Moana Center outing, Pixie—who was probably around 3 at the time—managed to get her head caught between the metal bars of a railing.

Pixie's panicked cries drew the kind of big crowd I could only dream of getting at a wrestling match, along with the Honolulu Fire Department. Then, as one fireman approached her to help, the big man in the fireman's suit scared Pixie so badly that she yanked her head out of the bars herself. Crisis averted!

There were also those days when the crazy events at the Francis family home took their toll on me at the office. Some days when I came in to work to plan the week's matches, Lord Blears could tell immediately that I'd had another rough night. The telltale saddle bags under my bloodshot eyes were pretty clear evidence of one thing.

Blears would look at me, nod sympathetically, and simply say, "The monkey again?"

"Yeah. The damn monkey again," I'd say with a sigh.

My wife Arlene was a true animal lover. Not just dogs and cats and goldfish. All kinds of animals. Including exotics. Including monkeys.

So it was that we acquired a monkey named Jeannie at our house on Ulupii Street in Olomana.

I remain convinced today that Jeannie was the meanest monkey on the planet.

I have no idea what hardships Jeannie the monkey endured as a child. I cannot fathom what terrible sad turns of fate darkened Jeannie's outlook on the world. But for whatever reasons she had, Jeannie was nasty and angry, and was never afraid to let us know it.

There was only one person Jeannie could actually tolerate. That was—no surprise—Arlene. Jeannie would sit on Arlene's shoulder for hours, calm, at peace, deceptively amiable.

But let Jeannie out when the kids were around, and our front yard at Ulupii Street would instantly turn into some sort of B-movie horror film.

All the kids would run shrieking from Jeannie. Jeannie would give chase, baring her nasty little monkey teeth and nipping at their fingers and toes. The kids would get a big thick blanket to throw over the crazed monkey, but Jeannie would just bite them right though the blanket.

And Jeannie's wrath wasn't saved for the Francis family exclusively. Jeannie lived in a giant eight-foot-tall cage in our garage, but occasionally, when we had dinner parties at the house, Arlene would let her adorable little pet out to greet the guests.

(*Her* adorable little pet. Certainly no one else's.)

Lord Blears and his gorgeous wife, Lee, were guests at our house for one of these parties, when Arlene Unleashed the Beast.

First, Jeannie the MFH (Monkey from Hell) scampered up and peed on the shirt of a guest of ours in from Oregon. Then Jeannie made a beeline for Lee Blears.

Lee had beautiful, long dark hair cascading over her shoulders. Jeannie managed to get herself completely ensnarled in that hair, as poor Lee ran screaming around our yard with a monkey on her head, and Lord Blears gave chase in vain. That party ended very early.

Not much later, Jeannie managed to escape her cage in the garage. (I can't imagine who might have left the cage unlatched, to give Jeannie her freedom.) And, of course, it fell to me to go recapture her.

It wasn't a pretty picture: Gentleman Ed Francis, former Junior Heavyweight Champion of the World, founder and president of Mid-Pacific Promotions, weekly fixture on KGMB-TV and icon to wrestling fans throughout the Islands, chasing a monkey down Ulupii Street in Olomana.

Sure, I had skills as a wrestler. But they were no match for a crazed monkey in the open field.

Jeannie bounded through yards and houses, and ended up on the roof of a neighbor's house. I ran home and grabbed a ladder and a blanket. By now there was an animal-control wagon cruising the neighborhood. Someone had called them about a monkey on the loose.

I had to snag Jeannie before animal control got her. So I ran back to the neighbor's house, blanket in hand, and climbed my ladder.

Billy and Ed inside the Civic Auditorium. Opposite: Ed "Sonny" Francis, Jr., surfing on Oahu's North Shore in 2010.

A FAMILY AFFAIR

Jeannie couldn't care less. She was playing on the roof, paying no attention to me.

Our neighbor came out of his house to get the mail, and Jeannie leaned over the rain gutter above him, trying to grab his hair as he passed beneath her. But all he saw was some crazed neighbor with a blanket on a ladder leaning up against his house.

Jeannie bounded away with one effortless jump, and the chase continued.

I stalked Jeannie through the neighborhood till the sun began to set. By then the neighbors across the street were having a little party. I looked over and there was Jeannie, in a tree in the yard right next to the party house.

Quietly, with as much stealth as I could muster, I crept over and started climbing the tree. I didn't want the partygoers to see me. Or Jeannie.

I got about halfway up the tree, within a couple of arm's lengths of Jeannie, and she jumped directly over me to the branches below. Off she went with an attention-getting rustle of leaves. At the party below me, the guests all looked up, and none of them could figure why their neighbor was climbing a tree at sundown. (Funny. He always seemed like such a nice, normal guy.)

Exhausted, embarrassed, defeated, I crossed the street and headed home.

There was Jeannie, sitting on our front stoop. I picked her up and put her back in her cage.

In time, Arlene, and the kids as they grew, began to find jobs and pastimes of their own, far from my wrestling world. Arlene's duties as a stay-at-home Mom began to change as the kids got older, so she went back to school in the nursing field and began to fill her time as a nurse.

When my son Russ got older he became an avid pilot. After his pro football and wrestling days were done, Russ ultimately charted a professional path for himself up in the air as a pilot and air-charter owner.

Russ had first learned to fly in Eugene, Oregon, and he used a $25,000 signing bonus he'd gotten to lure him to the World Football League to buy his first plane, a single-engine Beechcraft Sierra.

148

As Russ was just getting his air businesses off the ground, he also had a small airline with some Beech Queen airplanes that could take nine passengers in each. Together we would fly handfuls of wrestlers to their matches on the outer islands.

One of these trips involved the crazy French Canadian wrestler Maurice "Mad Dog" Vachon, plus Pampero Firpo, the guy everyone knew ("Ohhhh yeahhhh!") as The Missing Link, and some others. Just for fun, I'd also brought along my youngest son, Sonny. Russ was piloting one plane carrying some of the wrestlers, and I was in a second plane with another pilot.

Our group headed over to Kauai and put on our matches there for an appreciative crowd. But when we were done, our plane had just gotten a short distance out of Lihue Airport when we ran head-on into a huge thunderstorm.

Our planes were getting rocked pretty badly, and as the streak lightning crackled across the plane wings, the flashes illuminated the cabin inside. I could see the eyes of Vachon, Link and everyone else, wide as giant rice balls.

Before the storm knocked out the electrical systems in our plane, we heard a report on our radio that the storm had taken out the radar at the airport in Honolulu. Now I was using a flashlight to shine on the instrument panel, trying to make the best of it.

We zigzagged on toward Honolulu, two small aircraft just trying to hold it together, but with every pitch and toss of the planes in the storm our hearts all but stopped. We all held our collective breath and it got very quiet in my plane. It was truly white-knuckle time. The only sounds we heard were the sputtering of the engine and the cracking of the lightning outside.

Finally, The Missing Link looked at me with that wide, grisly, bearded mug of his, and said in his funny accent, "Mr. Francis, my hands are sweating. Are we going to go down?"

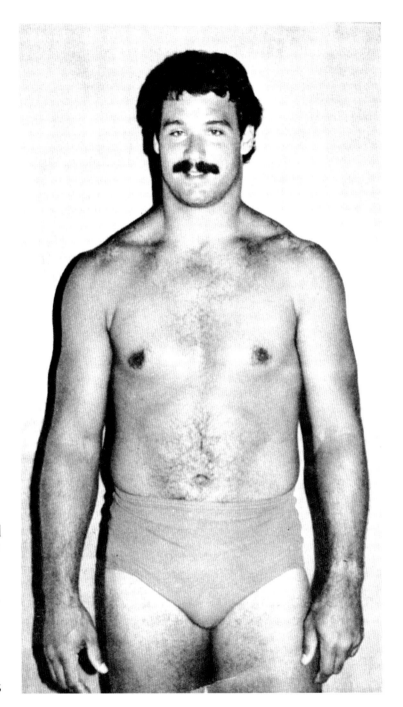

149

Truth be told, my hands were sweating too. I was well aware that small planes under siege by storms fell out of the sky all the time. My son Russ was on the stick in one, and my young son Sonny was in our group in the air. What if the storm actually proved too much for us? We turned both planes around and headed back to Kauai. It was a wise decision. We made it to the ground safely and spent the night there while we waited out the weather. But times in the air like that made it very difficult for me to talk big strong wrestlers into getting on board tiny little interisland planes.

Russ also flew celebrities around the Islands in his private chartered planes. He flew many frequent VIP visitors to the Islands who didn't want to fly commercial. Among his celebrity clientele were Carol Burnett, Dom DeLuise and many other big stars, including Burt Reynolds.

On one of Burt's trips to Hawaii, Russ had flown him to and from the outer islands and was taking him on a little ground tour of Oahu. But Burt made the mistake so many visitors make—he entered the water out at Makapuu and wasn't ready for the rip current.

Literally within seconds, Reynolds was swept away from shore and carried out precariously close to the pounding surf and the jagged lava-rock coastline. Russ saw that Burt was in trouble. Luckily, Russ was a powerful swimmer, since he'd grown up surfing. He hit the water, made his way to Burt and pulled him back in to safety. Reynolds couldn't stop thanking Russ for saving his life.

All of Russ's devotion to airplanes and to flying later led us to open a business together in Boulder City, Nevada. We'd gotten word that they were looking to open a small airport there and, with some wrangling of financial support, we got involved in opening it.

From there we started with a single airplane—a little Cessna 172—and began air-ferrying passengers for sightseeing trips above the Grand Canyon. The business grew slowly, with Russ and I both flying and upgrading our certifications. We hired more pilots and brought in more planes, until at one point in our operation we had as many as a dozen aircraft under our wing.

Our family's love of both Hawaii and small airplanes intersected again when Russ ran for a Hawaii Congressional seat in 2000. Russ rented a small twin-engine Beechcraft plane to make his barnstorming, whistle-stop campaign

Bill, Ed and Russ Francis in Eugene, Oregon, in the 1970s. Opposite: Ed, Jr. on the motocross track at Kahuku, Oahu.

tour of the Islands, and I traveled with him for much of the time.

The view from that plane as we headed over to the Big Island, chasing whales as they played in the ocean below us, was something I'll never forget.

I've always said that I have a pipeline to God.

None of us can ever know—till we get to the other side—too much about God. But, in my mind, we all need to believe in something, or we have nothing.

And up in the air on that day, surveying the breathtaking beauty of Hawaii spreading itself out beneath us, I did, indeed, feel closer to God. This paradise, which Mark Twain described as "the loveliest fleet of islands that lies anchored in any ocean," has truly been touched by His hand. ◆

A FAMILY AFFAIR

The Francis boys at the family ranch in Pleasant Hill, Oregon, ca. 1972: (left to right) Russ, Jim, Bill, Ed, Sonny and Bob. Opposite: Russ on his farm in Vermont.

CHAPTER 18

Aloha to the Islands

Several factors contributed to the winding down of our wrestling operation in Hawaii in the mid- to late 1970s.

First on the list was my own involvement at the ranch I'd bought in Oregon, a beautiful, 150-acre spread at the foot of the Willamette Mountains.

I had always enjoyed Oregon. I'd become familiar with it when I wrestled up there for Don Owen, the man who lent me the $10,000 to start our operation in Hawaii.

(By the time I returned to the area to buy the ranch, I had, of course, long since paid Don Owen back in full, with my deepest gratitude. I was also happy to play host in Hawaii many times to Don and his family when they came over to visit.)

For several months, I split my time between the ranch and our home in Hawaii. Then, slowly, over time, family and focus moved to the ranch and its upkeep, and I was finding it more and more difficult to keep all the balls in the air for 50th State Big Time Wrestling.

Though Hawaii will always hold the most special place in my heart, at the time we had thoughts of retiring in Oregon. The ranch there offered much more space than we could ever afford in Hawaii and, for as long as I can remember, I was enamored of the cowboy "ropin' and ranchin'" lifestyle. I loved all the activities involved with

stabling and riding horses.

I ended up selling our house on Ulupii Street and moved my whole family to Oregon. We all rode horses and worked the ranch, and Russ even got into rodeos. The Francis family turned into cowboys and cowgirls.

Meanwhile, I was still flying back and forth to the Islands for the TV shows, and Lord Blears was handling the rest of the business when I wasn't there. It was a lot to expect of him, and I knew it couldn't continue that way.

Another big factor in the decline of 50th State Big Time Wrestling was the ultimate fate of one of my long-standing dreams in Hawaii: to build our very own wrestling arena on Oahu.

The grand old Civic Auditorium had received its death warrant. The HIC facility

153

was a shade too large for our purposes. It was used for a variety of other events and, of course, booking events there involved working with and paying fees to the City & County of Honolulu.

I'd always envisioned the day when we could have a facility built especially for us, to house wrestling, boxing, basketball and other sporting events, tailor-made for our needs.

I had paid to have some beautiful plans drawn up for our brand-new facility. I worked with state and city planners to map out the infrastructure for the roads providing access to the venue and its parking lot. I secured ample investors' funding to back the ambitious project.

The last step was to receive approval from a local government agency in order to green light the project. But after they received my proposal and reviewed it, my project manager came back and told me that the commissioners required an additional $250,000 fee, paid up front and in full to them, before they would approve it.

Opposite: After the Civic Auditorium was razed in 1974 to make way for a high-rise, a "sports restaurant" was opened on the building's ground floor to commemorate the old arena.

It was never made clear to me what the fee was for, and I couldn't justify the cost to our investors. So the project was killed, and my dream of our own facility in the Islands never came to pass.

With those plans falling away, and my attentions turning to the ranch across an ocean, it began to feel the writing was on the wall for our wrestling business in Hawaii.

But, without question, the proverbial straw that broke the camel's back was the shutting down of the Civic Auditorium.

It was long overdue. The grand old lady was showing her age every week. There were nights during our matches that the action had to be stopped, because (despite Velasco's hard work and care) chunks of the ceiling had fallen into the ring.

The house that had hosted so many of our greatest wrestling moments, and had showcased the greatest of Honolulu entertainment events over the past four decades, was becoming a health hazard and a dinosaur. Her time had come.

The closing of the Civic was, at the time, a nail in our coffin. Though we still had the HIC, those matches were just monthly affairs. It simply wasn't the same as our weekly matches from the Civic that supported the weekly TV shows and fed the appetites of our fans. The loss of the Civic for our weekly Wednesday-night matches meant no regular weekly show for KGMB, so our TV exposure wound down as well.

Then, as if it was meant to be, a former wrestler and wrestling promoter from New Zealand named Steve Rickard came to me and told me he wanted to buy my promotional rights for wrestling in the Hawaii region.

It was a big step. It was what I'd known, what I'd built, what I'd devoted all my energy to, every waking hour of every day, for more than 15 years.

But I had a little talk with myself. I said: The Civic's gone. HIC rent is high. The box office is down. TV wrestling viewers are down. Wrestlers' fees are up. Nothing lasts forever. It's time to go.

My first stop after that was a heart-to-heart with my constant co-conspirator for so many years, Lord Tally Ho Blears.

Lord and I sat down and I told him what I'd decided. But Blears had seen this coming for quite some time; it wasn't an overnight thing. Blears had always been very thrifty with his money. He had gotten help from a builder—the same one I used to help build our house on the ranch in Oregon—to build him and his wife, Lee, a nice A-frame home out in Makaha.

Blears told me he completely understood. He'd be fine.

My deal with Rickard for the rights to my operation involved some cash, plus the promise of an ongoing consultancy fee for me. I was to continue to help him by working with the TV people to keep his presence there and keep the wrestling in front of the fans.

While I had originally bought the wrestling-promotion rights from Al Karasick for $10,000, I agreed to sell the rights to Rickard for $50,000, plus an additional, secondary $30,000 fee and $1,500 per month for my consulting services.

From where I sat, that all sounded great.

It didn't work out that way.

Shortly after we made the deal, another pair of figures loomed on the scene. It was a married couple: our good wrestler friend, Peter Maivia, and his wife, Lia.

Maivia had been in our wrestling family for years, and I respected him greatly. His wife, Lia, however, was a very driven woman, and was obsessed with advancing and promoting the Samoan culture.

For whatever reason, prompted primarily by Lia, the Maivias saw this transitional time of wrestling promotion in Hawaii as an opportunity for them. They boldly staked their own claim

155

to promoting wrestling in Hawaii—without paying any fees—and essentially intimidated Rickard into leaving the Islands.

After Ed sold his Hawai'i wrestling rights, wrestler Peter Maivia promoted the sport in the Islands until his death in 1982.

(Not long after I'd left Hawaii, I returned on a visit. Lia Maivia called me and threatened harm to my family if I considered resurrecting our wrestling-promotion business. She was a woman blinded by ambition and driven to succeed at all costs, by any means.)

With the intervention of the Maivias, I never saw much of the agreed-upon money from Rickard. The Maivias promoted wrestling in Hawaii into the 1980s, until Vince McMahon's World Wrestling Federation became the overriding force in professional wrestling nationwide. The days of wrestling in Hawaii—tailored specifically for Hawaii fans—were all but over.

Our glory days of 50th State Big Time Wrestling from the early 1960s into the late 1970s came at a very special time in the wrestling business. It was a time when regional promoters like me all respected each other's operations, and created our own unique product for our fans.

For the most part, that day of the regional wrestling promoter, running his own territory and serving the local culture within its boundaries, has come and gone.

True, there is still a variety of wrestling promoters working around the U.S. But the marketing genius of Vince McMahon has built his operation into the WalMart of the wrestling trade, and with good reason.

Just as with our business in Hawaii and with all successful pro-wrestling empires, it begins with the wrestlers. From the start, Vince built a remarkable stable of memorable characters whose stories and exploits drew the fans in. He had the enormous wisdom early on to build his business on the broad shoulders of powerful wrestlers like Hulk Hogan and Steve Austin, Roddy Piper and The Rock.

Their battles and exploits generated big fan reaction, big money and big TV contracts that let Vince gobble up the smaller mom-and-pop operations around the country. All the top wrestlers gravitated toward Vince and his WWF—including many of the guys who wrestled for us in Hawaii—because that's where the money was.

(In fact, at one point, my son Russ wrestled for Vince in one of his giant "Battle Royals." Too bad Russ didn't tell me about it in advance, because I would have negotiated a bigger paycheck for him!)

Certainly another masterstroke of McMahon's was creating monster pay-per-view events for his wrestlers and their fans. With the right timing and marketing, all of McMahon's "Wrestlemania" events generated a fan feeding frenzy, and the money came pouring in.

That money—and more—is still there today in McMahon's operation. Each generation of Vince's stars brings the same top game. They're big, they're loud, they're fearless and they're entertaining.

Vince has had the further wisdom to call his product "sports entertainment." By recognizing that his sport is also entertainment—the "show" in show business—McMahon frees up his own hand to control how the matches are presented.

It has made a world of difference in his success. It has helped him avoid some of the kinds of regulations and oversight that I, too, had to dodge in Hawaii, when the Hawaii State Boxing Commission wanted to license our wrestlers.

The most loyal wrestling fans don't care whether you call it pure sport or sports entertainment. They just want to see the action and follow the wild characters. McMahon knows how to provide the product his audience wants to see. That's all that matters.

Many have sounded the death knell of pro wrestling with the advent of the UFC (Ultimate Fighting Championship) and mixed-martial-arts

competition. Though I don't own a crystal ball (but, wow, how I wish I had one back in the day!), I fully expect that McMahon will get into the mixed-martial-arts business, because it could hugely benefit from his skill at identifying, promoting and marketing big personalities with true star quality.

McMahon is a shrewd businessman and a visionary. I don't think it'll be long before we see UFC matches staged with the trademark McMahon flair for the dramatic, complete with larger-than-life mixed-martial artists who are great showmen as well as fearless warriors in the ring.

The brutal, angry world of the UFC is pure blood sport, and its tremendous success might be a comment on our 21st-century tastes and tolerances in society. Competitors are truly out for blood, and the matches feed a hunger for the kill not unlike that of the Romans in gladiator days.

I'd like to believe there will continue to be a place for a kinder, gentler brand of competition in the ring. Pro wrestling has always been as much about the show as the ultimate outcome. The end game is not primarily about the actual physical harm or the incapacitating of an opponent.

In the matches we put on for so many years in Hawaii, the personalities, the interviews, the posturing and the grudges made the competitors feel like family to the fans. Yes, pro wrestlers work hard, and they get hurt. But I remain convinced today that the Hawaii fans turned out for the rivalries, not the injuries. I'd like to believe that fans of pro wrestling will keep turning out and cheering, in Hawaii and elsewhere, for many generations to come. ◆

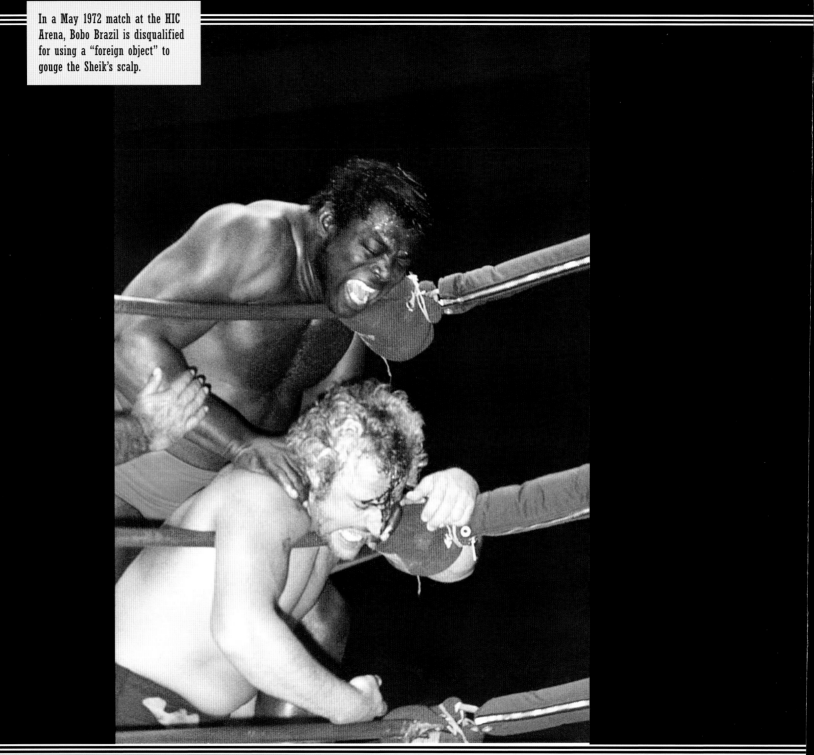

In a May 1972 match at the HIC Arena, Bobo Brazil is disqualified for using a "foreign object" to gouge the Sheik's scalp.

A Lasting Legacy

One of the greatest elements of personal pride in my life is the honor of being considered by so many in the Islands as a true kamaaina.

On the surface, of course, the honor might seem misplaced. After all, I was born and raised on the streets of Chicago, and traveled the Mainland as a wrestler for hire before settling in Hawaii.

But just as I felt that I somehow fit in the moment my feet touched Hawaii shores, even today, so many years later, our many friends and fans in the Islands continue to support me, to embrace me and to welcome me and my family back as their own.

Maybe it's because I was on TV every week for so many years, in people's living rooms. They felt they knew me. As I studied their reactions to our matches in the arenas, I certainly felt that I knew them.

Maybe it's also because I raised my family right alongside theirs, sitting at high-school sports events together in Kailua, watching the kids compete.

Maybe most of all it's because we shared something unique together in those crazy days of 50th State Big Time Wrestling. We shared the Civic and the HIC. We shared the matches on the outer islands and at Schofield and Pearl Harbor. We shared the weekly insanity of those locker-room interviews.

At the time, I barely had the chance to enjoy them, because every day I was worrying about tomorrow: Who should we put on the card for Wednesday night? Will a little sprinkling of rain keep the fans away? How is Ripper Collins going to insult me on live television this week? And … where is my wife's damn monkey?

Now, with the advantage of hindsight and more than a few intervening years, I can see with very sharp focus just how special those Hawaii wrestling years were, both for me personally, and for the fans we entertained.

Hawaii was a young state then, full of pride and promise. Yes, there were undeniably those cultural differences within the Islands' population, and a few quietly simmering tensions, which we framed and magnified for dramatic effect inside the ring. Good drama needs conflict.

What I saw, however, with just a quick glance at the faces of the fans sitting side by side at our matches, night after night, week after week, taught me something very different, something important.

These fans were all ages: kids, dads, moms, grandpas and tutus. They were Hawaiian and Chinese, Filipino and Samoan, Japanese and Portuguese, Korean and haole. They shouted together, they gasped together, they laughed together and

they left the Civic or the HIC with smiles on their faces, abuzz about what they'd just seen.

After every match, before I hurried back to my desk to strategize with Lord Blears and to fret about the next week's show, I stood amid the crowd that streamed out of the venue and listened to the fans.

Here's what I heard:

"I tol' you Iaukea could take Barend! No way Curtis goeen' lose to dat pretty boy!"

"You saw da guy Mad Dog Mayne chew up da glass? Ho, da freekah is crazy!!"

"What, Maiava and Missing Link? Bes' tag team, garans ball-barans, brah! Nobody goeen' beat dem!"

"Eh, you wen' spock Meestah Francis whippeen' Rippah wit' da belt? Ho, da fat haole get da kine welts on da back, brah!!"

The fans cared. They were invested, even if only for a little while. They went home to their families and their own lives in Hawaii—but, with a little planning on our part and a whole lot of luck, they'd return the following week to invest again in our over-the-top, over-the-top-ropes brand of entertainment.

The concept of ohana has always been a very powerful force in Island cultures. Nothing is stronger than the bond of family. In a very real sense, what we presented to the fans in Hawaii was the chance to be part of another kind of ohana.

Granted, our family of wrestlers was wildly dysfunctional, generally unpredictable and always at war. But, by following the exploits of Curtis and Neff, Ripper and Johnny, Steamboat, Andre, Muraco and the rest—all under the watchful eyes of their reluctant "parents," Lord Blears and me—Hawaii fans got a sense of belonging to something exciting, filled with energy.

Through their loyalty and support, the Hawaii fans gave me and my young family a roof over our heads (sometimes with a monkey on it) and food on the table. I will forever feel an enormous debt of gratitude to the fans of Hawaii for their many years of devotion.

To repay this debt, I plan to return to Hawaii someday soon, to live in the Islands full time and to give back. I am laying plans to combine my love for the people of Hawaii and my love of horses, by launching a nonprofit working, teaching ranch as a learning destination for Hawaii's underprivileged children.

Many—perhaps most—kids in Hawaii have never experienced the joy I know of working with horses, of racing at a full gallop across the Island countryside. It is a breath-catching thrill that creates memories to last a lifetime.

Plans for our nonprofit horse ranch are still very much in the preliminary fundraising stages. But I can easily envision the day when kids in Hawaii of all ages and socioeconomic backgrounds will get the opportunity to enjoy their days at the ranch—riding, roping and laughing.

In this small way, I hope to leave a lasting legacy for wrestling fans in Hawaii, a small "thank you" for our incredible, stressful, wonderful years together. I will make the ranch happen for the kids—because I've done tougher things.

Hell, I've wrestled a bear. ✦

A LASTING LEGACY

Index

ED FRANCIS VS. FRED BLASSIE

SPECIAL EVENT | TITLE MATCH

BABA vs SHEIK | CURRY vs QUINN

★★★★★★★★★★★★★★★★★★★★★★★★

INTERNATIONAL ALL STAR WRESTLING

WED **HIC ARENA** AUG. 2ND

623 LBS. HAYSTACKS 623 LBS.

HAYSTACKS & JOHNNY BAREND
VS.
SHEIK & FRED BLASSIE

PROMOTER ED FRANCIS PRESENTS AT....

HON. INTER. CENTER

WORLDS TEAM CHAMPIONSHIP

(BIGGEST MATCH IN HISTORY)

THE SHEIK & JOHNNY BAREND
ACCOMPANIED BY THE WEASEL
VS
RAY STEVENS & PETER MAIVIA
WORLDS CHAMPIONS

★★★★★★★★★★★★★★★★★★★★

Collins vs Steamboat ★ SHIBUYA vs PEDRO

★★★★★★★★★★★★★★★★★★★★

HAWAIIAN C
GENE KINISKI

GIRLS ★ WA

MISS VACHON

PLUS—FRAN
BOAT PSNUKA
2.50 ● 3.50 ● 4.5

★★★★★★★★★★★

INTERNATIONAL A

WED. **HIC**

N. A. CHA

FRED BLASSIE V

SHEIK & FAROU
THE WEASEL

ED FRANCIS V
EXECUTIONEF

2ND TA